MW00324605

Soldier On

Soldier On

My Father, His
General, and the Long
Road from Vietnam

TRAN B. QUAN

TEXAS TECH UNIVERSITY PRESS

Copyright © 2021 by Texas Tech University Press

All rights reserved. No portion of this book may be reproduced in any form or by any means, including electronic storage and retrieval systems, except by explicit prior written permission of the publisher. Brief passages excerpted for review and critical purposes are excepted.

This book is typeset in Crimson Text. The paper used in this book meets the minimum requirements of ANSI/NISO Z39.48-1992 (R1997). ∞

Designed by Hannah Gaskamp

Library of Congress Cataloging-in-Publication Data
Names: Quan, Tran B., 1974– author.
Title: Soldier On: My father, His General, and the Long Road from Vietnam / Tran B. Quan.
Description: [Lubbock, Texas]: Texas Tech University Press, [2021] | Includes bibliographical references and index. | Summary: "The story of a South Vietnamese officer who smuggles his family out of the country toward the end of the Vietnam War, as told by his daughter. Forty years after the departure, the officer reconnects with a respected general, Tran Ba Di, during a family road trip to Key West, Florida."—Provided by publisher.

Identifiers: LCCN 2021005430 (print) | LCCN 2021005431 (ebook)
ISBN 978-1-68283-097-0 (paperback) | ISBN 978-1-68283-098-7 (ebook)

Subjects: LCSH: Vietnamese—United States—Biography. | Vietnamese Americans—Biography. | Quan, Le, 1948– | Quan, Le, 1948—Family. | Di, Tran Ba, 1931– | Vietnam (Republic). Quân lực—Officers—Biography. | Political prisoners—Vietnam—Biography. | Political refugees—Vietnam—Biography.
Classification: LCC E184.V53.Q35 2021 (print) | LCC E184.V53 (ebook) | DDC 973/.04959220092 [B]—dc23
LC record available at https://lccn.loc.gov/2021005430
LC ebook record available at https://lccn.loc.gov/2021005431

Printed in the United States of America
21 22 23 24 25 26 27 28 29 / 9 8 7 6 5 4 3 2 1

Texas Tech University Press
Box 41037
Lubbock, Texas 79409-1037 USA
800.832.4042
ttup@ttu.edu
www.ttupress.org

For Dad

Contents

Illustrations — ix

Foreword — xi

1   Key West — 3

2   The Rascal — 16

3   The Cadet — 30

4   The First Imprisonment — 36

5   The Young Officer — 43

6   The Mission — 50

7   Respite — 60

8   Death — 69

9   The Soldier's War — 75

10   The General's War — 81

11   The Advisors — 90

12   The Fall — 104

13   The Second Imprisonment   —   120

14   Prison Camp   —   131

15   Survival   —   136

16   The Escape   —   150

17   Refugee Camp   —   157

18   America   —   170

19   Fortitude   —   178

20   Texas   —   192

21   The Reagan Letter   —   206

22   Seventeen Years   —   214

23   The American Dream   —   222

24   N&T Seafood   —   228

25   The Three Letters   —   239

26   Honest Labor   —   244

27   The Destination   —   251

Acknowledgments   —   257

Bibliography   —   259

Index   —   263

Illustrations

15   Oversea Highway, Orlando to Key West, summer 2015

17   Author's father at ten years old

33   Author's father reading a letter from home, Thu Duc Military Academy, 1968

38   Author's father, his friend Thanh Du, General Di, author's mother, Cousin Hung, and Hung's wife Hoang, Florida rest area

47   Major Di awarding medal to village militiaman, 1963

51   Author's father looking out on the grounds of the ARVN 16th Regiment, 1970

65   Author's parents celebrating their engagement, 1971

67   Author's parents honeymooning in Da Lat, Vietnam

97   General Di sharing meal with American advisors, including Captain McFarland, 1963

159   Author's parents in front of hut in Laem Sing Refugee Camp, Thailand

180   Grothen family and author's family sledding in Hastings, Nebraska

181   Author, author's father, and John Deere tractor, Nebraska, 1980

212   General Di's letter to Ronald Reagan, 1981

224   Cousin Hung and wife, Hoang, author's mother, author, author's sister, author's father, General Di, John Pennekamp Coral Reef State Park, Key Largo

226   Author's family home

232   N&T Seafood Market, Houston

242   Author with captain's bars, May 25, 2002

246   General Di pedaling snack pushcart, Orlando's Splendid China Amusement Park, 1993

254   Author in Key West with General Di and author's father

255   Author's father and General Di, Key West, 2015

Foreword

THE LITERATURE OF THE Vietnam War is vast but conspicuously sparse in two important areas: assessments of American advisory assistance to the South Vietnamese and accounts by the Vietnamese themselves. As regards the latter category, Tran Quan's fine memoir is a valuable contribution to our knowledge, understanding, and appreciation of the Vietnamese diaspora, especially in America.

Born in South Vietnam during the last stage of the war, Tran came to America at just five years of age with her parents and a six-year-old brother. They in effect escaped from their homeland, becoming "boat people," after her father had suffered three years in a communist prison camp. A very difficult path still lay ahead of them. She tells their story without self-pity or sugarcoating.

Tran Quan is intelligent, observant, and grateful for the new life she and her family found in America. And she is an extraordinary researcher, tenacious and relentless, basically "extracting" from her father Le Quan and his wartime commander the details of their ordeals as prisoners in the so-called "reeducation" camps, Major General Tran Ba Di for an incredible seventeen years.

Tran's book also demonstrates her enormous energy and dedication. She served as a US Army Medical Corps captain for a number of years. This represented an extraordinary accomplishment on her part. When still a little girl—as she and her family were trying to adjust to life in a country where they knew neither the language nor the customs—Tran had considerable trouble in school. Her father drew her to him. "I believe in you," he said.

He was right to do so. Late one night, many years later, Tran showed her father three letters. The first informed her that she would be graduating from college magna cum laude. The second was an acceptance to medical school. The third, from the US Army, told her she was being awarded a scholarship that would pay her medical school expenses in return for four years of service as a captain in the Army Medical Corps. The sharing of those letters must have constituted an event of almost unbelievable triumph and gratification for both father and daughter.

For the past decade, Tran has been medical director of the Richmond State Supported Living Center, part of a Texas network assisting individuals with intellectual and developmental disabilities. While carrying out these demanding duties she simultaneously researched and wrote this moving account of her family and its travails and triumphs.

It thus seems quite fitting to me that Tran Quan completed her book and found a publisher during the zodiacal Year of the Rat. I have considerable sympathy for the Rat. He lives a hard life and never gives up. I hope Tran will be flattered, not offended, by the comparison.

Tran's story is perfectly suited for Texas Tech University Press, exemplifying as it does the under-reported but inspiring story of how perhaps a million South Vietnamese left their homeland after it was overrun by the communists and made their way to America, where they have by dint of hard work, family loyalty, and ability made new lives for themselves and enriched our culture.

LEWIS SORLEY, PHD

Soldier On

CHAPTER 1

Key West

WHILE THE WAIT STAFF wriggled between the seats of the packed Orlando restaurant and customers chattered away enjoying their meals, a silver-haired Vietnamese man in his early sixties quietly cleared the dirty dishes from the empty tables. Even though it was his first month on the job, he worked fast, scraping food off the plates and stacking them into meticulous towers. His tanned, sinewy arms moved back and forth with precision. He surveyed a table and saw a half-eaten trout, grilled ribs with chunks of meat still on the bones, and clumps of warm rice left on plates. His heart sank as he emptied the leftover food into a garbage bin. For a moment, he thought about how for seventeen years he ate mostly cassava roots and drank dirty well water in the jungle prisons of Vietnam. The starchy, bland roots settled in his stomach like a puddle of paste. Sometimes he went to bed with an angry belly that growled from days without food.

A child from the next table knocked over a glass of soda. The man reached for a clean towel and wiped the spill. The father scolded his son without looking at the Vietnamese man, who gave the little boy an understanding smile before the child's eyes lowered with embarrassment. The little boy reminded the man of his youngest son who was now an adult. The seventeen years he spent locked up in the concentration camp had stolen birthdays and celebrations from his children—now all grown.

The man moved on to the next table, focused on his work, oblivious to the sounds of clattering dishes and silverware and the conversations around him. Sometimes he would find personal items left behind, like a wallet, which he would hand to the restaurant manager without opening. It was not the first time he found money that did not belong to him. Politicians and businessmen in Vietnam had delivered envelopes of cash to his office years before in order to gain influence. And just like before, he returned the money—untouched.

When the tables were cleared, he headed for the kitchen to empty the trays. He saw the kitchen dishwasher, a stocky middle-aged woman, struggling to keep up with the sink full of dishes that piled up faster than she could wash them. Without being asked, the man rolled up his sleeves and started scrubbing the dishes while she rinsed. She gave him a tired smile and said, "Thank you, *Anh Ba*. You are a kind gentleman."

He routinely introduced himself as "Anh Ba," which in Vietnamese translates to "Second Brother." It was the folksy nickname that he carried with him from his army days. Vietnamese customarily call each other "brother," "sister," "aunt," or "uncle," even if they are strangers. His coworkers assumed that the name was a reference to his birth order. They did not know that "Second Brother" referred to the two stars that he wore on his military uniform. They did not know that pre-1975, over nineteen years before he started working at the Orlando restaurant in 1994, he had a staff that waited on him. Personal drivers and helicopter pilots delivered him to battlefields, which he often visited to check on the welfare of his troops. Secretaries and assistants helped organize his days, even though he was self-disciplined and did not like the fuss of a large entourage. Even with cooks to prepare lavish meals, he preferred simple dishes and ate the same meals that his soldiers ate.

To his troops in the Army of the Republic of Vietnam (ARVN) in 1971 he was known as Major General Tran Ba Di. He commanded the ARVN's 9th Infantry Division, with over 10,000 soldiers. If he could visit and talk with every soldier in his division, he would, and he tried to do so. One soldier in the division knew well the affection the troops had for General Di. This soldier, my father, never forgot the impression the general made on him when he was a young first lieutenant.

NINE HUNDRED MILES AWAY, in Texas, on a mid-morning in 1990, my father stood on the assembly line at work. Dad diligently assembled the electronic parts that rolled past him. But the urge for a cigarette break to relax and to crack a few jokes with his friends made it hard for him to concentrate. He looked up at the company clock and saw that he had another hour to go. He couldn't wait; he needed his Marlboro. Dad signaled to his line leader, Kenneth, that he had to take a restroom break. Kenneth yelled, "Five minutes, Le!"

Kenneth, an African American man still in his twenties, supervised a group of fifteen workers who were at least a decade older. While Dad went to the restroom, Kenneth jumped on the assembly line and took his place. Kenneth's assembly lines had the fewest mistakes and produced the most products—when his crew worked.

Dad's coworkers knew where he was heading. A couple minutes later, a few of them joined him to light up their Marlboros, Camels, and Lucky Strikes inside the restroom. They let out roars of laughter while exhaling smoke as Dad imitated line leader Kenneth by curling in his lips as if he had missing front teeth like Kenneth.

When five minutes turned into ten minutes and still no sign of Dad or the other workers, Kenneth stopped the assembly line and went looking for his missing crew. He flung the bathroom door open and the men stubbed out their cigarettes and fanned the air with both hands. Kenneth hollered a few profane words, and they scattered back to work.

On his way out, Dad turned to Kenneth and made a face with his lips curled in like before and said, "Look, Kenneth, no teeth!" Kenneth's expression was dry, but he wasn't mad at Dad. The friends ribbed and jabbed each other at every opportunity. Still, Dad pulled back, sensing he might have crossed the line with his joke, "Sorry, Kenneth. Just playing with you."

Kenneth responded with a wide unbashful smile showing Dad his missing teeth and then held up a middle finger. He gave Dad a light punch in the gut and asked, "Lunch later?"

It was payday, which meant that they could splurge on burgers. Dad, Kenneth, and the same guys caught smoking sat down together and devoured their food. Dad ordered double meat with cheese and extra bacon on his burger and thought how blissful it would be if he had a cold beer to wash it down. The group continued their jokes and traded insults. No one teased Kenneth, except Dad.

When lunch ended, he turned to Kenneth and asked, "You coming over to eat with my family this weekend? Don't forget the cognac."

SOMETIMES, THE STRANGER WHO is helped becomes a lifelong friend. The friendship between Dad and Kenneth began one morning in 1983 during Dad's drive to work at Compaq computer company, where both men had recently been hired. Dad noticed a young African American man with calm, sleepy eyes who worked in the same department walking in the direction of the company. Kenneth carried a lunch bag in one hand and a small cloth rag in the other. He wiped his forehead with the rag as the early morning sun pounded his head and neck. He walked two miles from the bus stop and was still a mile away from Compaq.

Dad pulled up next to Kenneth in his 1975 Ford station wagon and asked, "You need a ride? We work on the same line. Get in."

Each morning, Kenneth took a bus from his apartment to the nearest bus stop at Compaq. He walked the rest of the way. Dad discovered that they lived near each other. He offered Kenneth a ride to and from work every day until Kenneth saved enough money to buy a used car. On those car rides, Dad learned that Kenneth had a college education and had moved to Houston from Louisiana without a family or a car.

Kenneth revealed, "I had a good job in Louisiana, working on the oil rigs. Made good money and spent it fast. Had too much fun, mostly in New Orleans. But I learned my lesson."

On their first payday, Kenneth asked Dad, "What kind of beer do you like?" Dad—knowing that neither could afford the drink at their current salary—replied, "I like cognac better." The next week, on the ride home, Kenneth handed Dad a brown paper bag. Inside was a bottle of rich, reddish-brown cognac. Dad looked at the paper bag a little surprised and embarrassed over this consequence of his joke, scratched his head, and said with a wide smile, "You come over to my apartment. Eat with my family. We cele-brate together."

Dad and Kenneth both started out doing the same jobs on the assembly line. But within a year, the company pro-moted Kenneth to team leader. Dad beamed with pride and bragged to the other workers about Kenneth. At the same time, he kept Kenneth grounded with his antics. The only change in their friendship once Kenneth became Dad's supervisor was the occasional verbal reprimand, "Hey, Le! No smoking on the assembly line or in the bathroom!"

Dad always looked for a reason to laugh and a new friend to join him. A cigarette and a can of beer made him even happier. His coworkers, however, did not know that he had grown up in wartime, fought in a war where he had to identify the bodies of dead childhood friends, and carried dying soldiers off battlefields. They did not know that he and his division commander, Major General Tran Ba Di, spent years in a communist hard labor camp—tor-tured and humiliated—after they lost their country in the Vietnam War.

DAD AND GENERAL DI resolutely forged ahead with their new lives in a new country after the war. They never talked much about their pasts, except for the occasional reminiscing with friends. Like the millions of other South Vietnamese expatriates who fled Vietnam, they came to America and steadily rebuilt their lives and raised their children.

Both men stayed the course and provided for their fami-lies until their retirement. General Di, eighteen years older than Dad, worked until he was seventy-six. In retirement, he kept his mind and body active with a regimented daily schedule. He swam and exercised at the YMCA each morn-ing and engaged his mind with books and puzzles in the afternoon. If he wasn't at home or at the YMCA, he went to the library and thumbed through stacks of books on history and geography. On Friday nights, he treated himself to a T-bone steak, his favorite American meal.

Dad also settled into a daily routine at retirement in 2014. He got up most mornings at 4 a.m. because nighttime sleep became harder. On a typical morning, he made himself a cup of coffee, walked out to the backyard, sat in an old kitchen chair, and lit a cigarette. He watched the early morning sky change from black to gray to the soft orange-pink of dawn. In the quiet solitude, he contently puffed away at his cigarette. His thoughts slowly drifted back forty-five years to a time much different from his present reality. His eyes appeared to focus on a line of flowering shrubs in the yard, but in his mind, he saw an unadorned helicopter attempt to land at the 16th Regimental Headquarters, where he was a twenty-three-year-old first lieutenant.

THE FIRST TIME DAD met General Di, the forty-one-year-old major general jumped out of the helicopter as soon as it touched the ground. The young, slender general had a thick head of jet-black hair that naturally stood on end. His smooth olive skin, bronzed by the sun, showed that he spent more time outside under the Southeast Asia sky than inside an office. Behind the sunglasses were sharp eyes that noted details quickly.

General Di made frequent, unannounced troop visits. When the regimental commanders organized a ceremonial welcome, General Di dismissed it and told them, "We are at war; it is not necessary." While other generals had gold stars painted on their helicopters and traveled with a team of five or six aides, General Di insisted that his vehicle and helicopter be kept simple. In place of assistants, he toured with just a briefcase-size portable radio communication device.

On this occasion, the regimental commander escorted General Di around the headquarters while giving him updates. It had been a day of brutal fighting, and the 16th Regiment sustained heavy casualties. Many of their wounded still lay on the battlefield, waiting for helicopters to evacuate them.

Dad pushed himself away from his office desk. He went outside and paced the grounds, wondering how he would be able to reach the wounded soldiers. His job was to evacuate the sick and injured from the frontline. Low on resources—that day and most days—the regiment did not have enough helicopters. Dad, caught up in his own thoughts, did not notice General Di walking toward him. When he recognized the general just a few feet away, he gave a quick salute.

General Di asked, "Young Brother, is there anything that you need?"

Surprised, relief flooded Dad's heart at being addressed in such a familiar way. He was used to orders barked at him that started with "Lieutenant!" or "You!" No senior officer had addressed him in such a gentle way. He mustered the courage to ask, "Sir, may I use your helicopter to evacuate the wounded soldiers still at the front?"

The regimental commander stood next to General Di with his mouth half open in disbelief over Dad's gutsy request. His mouth opened wider when General Di ordered his personal pilot to fly Dad to the awaiting troops.

The general's helicopter could carry up to twelve, but Dad pushed and squeezed as many soldiers in as fast as he could pull them from the rice paddy. Trails of mud and blood followed them onto the helicopter. When the last soldier was loaded, the pilot opened the throttle and the chopper blades spun with increasing speed until the craft lifted off the ground. The wind force created by the chopper flattened the lush green stalks of rice. Dad felt the knock of bullets ricochet off the helicopter as it rose into the air. He knew that Viet Cong guerrillas hiding in the tree lines were taking their last shots at them.

The noise from the engine and spinning rotor blades could not drown out the screams of soldiers bleeding from bullets still lodged inside them. Dad listened to them bellow, "Lieutenant! It hurts so bad!" He didn't know how to respond. The only relief he could offer was to say nothing and allow the wounded to vent their anguish. He couldn't decide which was worse, hearing their cries or the popping sounds of artillery from below, aimed at them. He could smell their misery from the stench of body odor mixed with the metallic essence of blood. The sour tang of the men's vomit that permeated through the cabin made it worse.

The evacuation left General Di's pristine helicopter saturated with mud, blood, vomit, and bullet holes. When Dad returned, he apologized and offered to hose the chopper off.

General Di patted Dad's shoulder and told him, "No need, Young Brother. Take care of my soldiers." There would be subsequent meetings between Dad and General Di, but those words sustained Dad throughout the war and after.

DAD SNAPPED BACK TO the present when he heard the back door open and saw me approaching. He tried to hide the cigarettes and looked innocently at me. His doctors and family pleaded with him to stop smoking, but it was a fifty-year-old habit that Dad was not ready to give up. I whiffed the lingering scent of tobacco but didn't say anything. I wanted to enjoy the peaceful quiet of morning, sitting next to him.

I am my father's daughter. We look alike and laughed at the same jokes.

I was the only one of his four children to join the military. He hung the American flag in front of his house for an entire year after I was commissioned as a captain in the US Army.

When I called him during my first week at basic training and complained about not having enough time to iron my uniform and polish my boots, he drove three hours from Houston to San Antonio to my Officer Basic Course (OBC).* He waited another three hours until I was released from class. He took one look at my scuffed boots and shook his head, even though he was never a spit-and-polish soldier. He warmed my can of shoe polish with his lighter to soften the wax, took out a rag, scooped out a small dollop of polish, and rubbed the black wax in a circular motion until the dull surface shined. I watched him hunched over, shining my boots. With a warm feeling inside I thought, *No one would ever drive three hours just to polish my Army boots, except my father.* After he was satisfied with one pair of boots, I handed him a second pair.

He traveled to other Army posts—Fort Hood, Fort Polk, and Camp Casey, South Korea—as I progressed through my military service. He would always leave me with a pair of polished boots and an ironed uniform before he went home.

When Dad retired, I left the Army because I missed home and him. Most mornings I found him at his usual spot. I planted myself next to him on another mismatched kitchen chair with a ripped seat. Dad had a hard time parting with his possessions as he got older. Content in silence, I sat with him until he spoke.

Dad started, "You know the general I've told you about? I talked to him the other day. He lives in Florida now. How about you plan a trip for us to Florida?" If my father wanted to go to Antarctica, I would find a way to make that happen. A trip from Texas to Florida was easy.

---

* Now Basic Officer Leader Course (BOLC), the entry-level course designed to produce Army commissioned officers, some of whom will be assigned to the Army Medical Department (AMEDD).

DAD SAT IN THE rented Orlando condominium, cracking his knuckles and checking the wall clock every five minutes, waiting for General Di. I had arranged and tagged along on this December 2014 trip to meet the general. It had been over forty years since the two men last met. Dad wondered how much time had changed them. Would he recognize his division commander?

General Di knocked on the door, which Dad opened to find the familiar sharp, smiling eyes, the wide, dimpled smile, and hearty laugh. General Di leaned on a cane to steady his balance, but everything else about the eighty-five-year-old general radiated a youthful, buoyant energy. He stood in front of Dad dressed in a pair of pressed pants with a crisp tucked-in short-sleeved shirt secured with a belt at the waist. His trimmed hair was cut in the familiar military style that he had worn years ago. Light bounced off his polished shoes. Dad knew that General Di hadn't dressed up just for him. This was the clean look the general consistently wore.

Dad straightened his faded tan shirt that Mom had begged him to throw away. He didn't like to wear new clothes, preferring old shirts to which he was sentimentally attached despite the holes and frayed edges. His gray mustache and thick mane of salt-and-pepper hair needed a trim.

Dad immediately saluted his division commander. General Di smiled and saluted back. For the next several hours, the two men traded stories of their postwar lives and early years in America. General Di spoke in a low, calm voice accompanied by frequent warm laughter. I sat in a corner, absorbing their stories.

When Dad reflected on the twists and turns of their lives since the war, I heard General Di quote Shakespeare, "All the world's a stage, and all the men and women merely players."

"Sir, what do you mean by that?" I asked, intrigued by his comment.

General Di answered, "During that part of my life, God had a role for me. I did my best in that role. Later, the role changed, but I am still who I am."

Dad did not want this visit with General Di to end. He invited the general to come along on a road trip with our family to Key West that his cousin in Florida had planned for the next summer. To Dad's delight, the general accepted.

Whether they knew it or not, Key West was a fitting destination. The southernmost point of the continental United States symbolized the end of a long journey. Approximately a hundred miles south lies one of the few remaining communist countries, Cuba. Forty-five years before and over 9,000 miles away, Dad and General Di first met during wartime and chaos in their native country, Vietnam. They fought against communism and were later tortured by their captors. From Key West in 2015, they could gaze toward the horizon from free soil, facing one of the last communist regimes.

I was born during wartime and fled my birth country with my parents before the age of five. The ideological conflict that resulted in the enormous exodus that swept my family from Vietnam to America loomed over me like an accepted fate during my youth. Even as life moved forward, Vietnam remained an elusive mystery to me. The many lingering questions that had accumulated in my mind over the years, which I pushed aside, came roaring back. What was the Vietnam War about from the standpoint of the South Vietnamese who fought it? What was it like to lose not just a home but a homeland? What drove my family's escape out of Vietnam? How did my parents, General Di, and the South Vietnamese refugees find the resiliency to persevere? To get my answers, I had to understand their journeys, and my father and General Di were ready to share them. The

On the Oversea Highway to Key West, summer 2015. (Courtesy of Tran B. Quan)

sights and senses came flooding back for both men as they sat side by side on the road trip, sharing the distant echoes of their past with the curious passengers. I listened, mesmerized by their accounts.

CHAPTER 2

The Rascal

DAD LEANED BACK IN his seat, yawned, and closed his eyes, preparing for a long nap as we started out on our trip.

"Daughter, you're in charge of navigation while Cousin Hung drives. Don't fall asleep," Dad ordered, then shut his eyes and let out a snore a few seconds later. Everyone voted that General Di should have the most comfortable seat, riding shotgun. But the general refused and instead offered it to me.

The ride along the Florida peninsula started from Orlando and hugged the western coastline toward Key West. Having lived in the state for forty years, Cousin Hung was our host and volunteered to drive. When he arrived in Florida from Vietnam, Cousin Hung did not want to settle anywhere else. There was no other place in America that he could grow his mango and coconut trees, which took root for decades in the backyard of his Melbourne, Florida home.

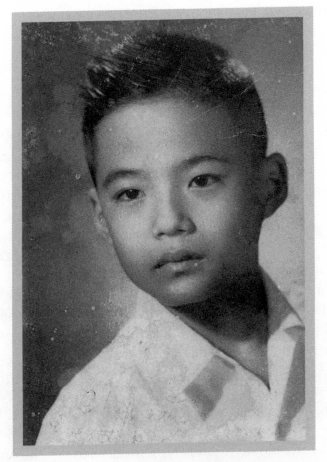

Dad at ten years old. (Courtesy of Tran B. Quan)

Occasionally, Dad opened his eyes to check the location and poke fun at his cousin. "Let your wife drive; she might get us there faster," Dad teased, eyes only half open. General Di, Mom, my youngest sister, Cousin Hung's wife, Dad's friend, and I all enjoyed the cousins' banter as we rolled toward Tampa.

Dad's eyes skimmed over a roadside billboard advertising a movie. He asked Cousin Hung, "Remember the trouble we got into as kids when we skipped school to go to the movies and ended up vandalizing movie posters?" Cousin

Hung nodded. Even though he was two years younger than Cousin Hung, Dad remembered that, as boys, he usually led excursions that got them both in trouble.

THEIR ESCAPADE STARTED OUT innocently enough when Dad and his gang of rascals made their way to town that day in 1960. They zipped past shops squeezed side by side along the narrow streets. The weathered concrete buildings constructed in the style of French architecture stood a few feet from the main drag where people in coned-shaped straw hats bicycled along while others were draped in the latest Western fashion. Pedestrians weaved past ox carts, motor scooters, and cars making their way across bustling streets. Merchants strolled outside to their shops' entrances with broom in hand to sweep and lay out their sun-ripened persimmons, dragon fruit, rambutans, and durians. Above the shops were balconies strung with lines where clothes flapped in the morning breeze.

Dressed in his school uniform of white shirt and black pants, twelve-year-old Dad untucked his shirt and ran toward the movie theater. He darted across the street past the cyclo drivers on their three-wheeled bicycle taxis. He caught a whiff of the rich aroma of stewed meats cooking in a broth of lemongrass and cinnamon waiting to feed hungry morning diners at the alley food stalls. Every open door to the shops and homes along the narrow alleyways was a slice of life in the town of Vinh Long.

Dad brushed past the neighborhood aunts and grandmothers standing over cauldrons of fragrant bubbling soups. The women stirred and mixed their broth. They gave him a smile showing their blackened teeth, stained from the daily chew of betel nut.

"Shouldn't you be in school?" they called out to him.

He ignored them and raced toward the movie theater with his buddies.

"Can we have a movie flyer?" the boys asked in unison. The manager impatiently shooed Dad and his gang of friends away. They couldn't fathom why he could not spare one flyer when there was a stack sitting on the counter. When they could not articulate their protest with words, they decided to have some fun. Dad found a bucket and helped his fellow mischief-makers fill it with dirt. He poured in water until they had a sticky mud paste. The boys then smeared their concoction across every posted movie flyer they found until the movie manager caught the culprits in the act. He chased them through the streets and narrow alleys. Down the boulevards they flew, knocking over street vendors in their path. The chase left a trail of straw baskets, filled with homegrown vegetables, scattered on the ground and angry merchants wanting to join the pursuit. The boys dispersed in different directions, looking for hiding spots. The theater manager eventually caught each one.

Dad sprinted down a row of shops toward his familiar hideout. He jumped inside a barrel behind an herbal medicine pharmacy and waited. The powerful scent of dried ginseng and licorice emanating from the glass jars of herbs, bark, and roots inside the shop reminded Dad of the strong brew of tea his mother drank to calm her nerves. The thought of her fury made him sweat even more inside the stifling barrel.

He didn't know it, but his friend's mom forced her son to reveal the main culprit's hideout. She felt that Dad was a bad influence on her child. She personally escorted the theater manager to Dad's hiding place. They yanked him out of the barrel and dragged him home to his mother.

BORN IN 1948 IN the town of Can Tho, Dad was the second oldest of ten children. But when his older brother died in toddlerhood, Dad became the oldest of nine. Grandmother Phuong had more trouble with him than her eight other children combined. She started chasing him around the house with a switch when he was not much older than six. When she caught him, she delivered several whacks to his backside. The sting to his rear, however, never deterred him from mischief—typically stealing fruit off the villagers' trees. From the age of eight to ten, Dad and a few of his bandit friends liked to swim across the river and scout the homes on the other side for trees ripe with nectarous tropical fruits like purple mangosteen. Dad's agile arms and legs propelled him across the river and hoisted him up the fruit trees. He dug his fingers into the hard, purple peel of the mangosteen to uncover a delicate, white juicy pulp that was both sour and sweet. Dad and his friends ate the fruits on site, leaving a trail of peels for the angry owners to find. When the boys caught sight of the homeowners, they jumped off the trees like a troop of monkeys and made a dash for the river.

Not long after, loud banging at the door followed. Grandmother Phuong became accustomed to the visits from irate neighbors coming to complain about Dad's pranks.

"He ate my precious fruits and left a mess in my yard!"

"He released my flocks of hens from their cages!"

"He gave my son a black eye!"

She listened politely and tried her best to suppress her boiling anger at the little boy who seemed to get into one scrape after another, despite her scolding and spanking. As soon as the neighbors left, she looked for the worn switch but could not find it or him.

As Dad got older, he outran and sometimes outwitted his mother. At age ten, he discovered how to pad his bottom with several layers of underwear and an extra pair of pants every time he got into trouble. She in turn got craftier and hogtied his arms and legs together with sturdy jungle vines to keep him from running. Even with his arms and legs bound together, he wriggled out of her grip and managed to hop away. On lucky occasions, he hopped right into the arms of his father who came home just in time from work. Grandfather Luong untied him and gave Grandmother Phuong a stern look.

His father never spanked and rarely used a harsh word against Dad. Grandfather Luong, a quiet man, chose his words and actions with care. Grandfather owned a brick factory and worked from dawn to dusk. He started the business with borrowed money and within two years paid off his debt. The brick factory stood on a riverbank only a few miles from their home. It provided essential supplies for the growing town and work for the villagers.

Dad obeyed his father without fear. He rarely saw Grandfather Luong display any anger except for one occasion, the memory of which he carried into adulthood. When he was ten, Dad took a stash of fireworks that he had been saving and decided to play a joke on the factory workers. With two packets of firecrackers stuffed inside his school bag, Dad made his way to the building that was surrounded by greenery, teeming with banana trees. He pushed back the smooth banana foliage and walked toward a cleared area of land on the riverbank where Grandfather's brick factory stood. The one-story building had rows of freshly made gray bricks stacked past his head. Dad studied the workers as they carried the sun-dried bricks inside to the beehive kiln, a chamber oven that stretched from the ground up to the twenty-foot ceiling. The kiln gave the bricks a final blast of heat to harden them. Dad wandered over to a group of workers cutting blocks of uncooked bricks from raw clay.

"What are you up to, rascal?" they asked. Dad gave them an innocent look and rambled toward the factory furnace. When no one was looking, he threw his packets of firecrackers into the furnace and dashed toward a corner to watch their reactions. A series of loud pops erupted that sounded like rapid gunfire. The workers scrambled for cover.

"We're under attack by the Viet Cong!" they screamed.

Grandfather Luong rushed out from his office to check out the commotion. He saw Dad holding his belly, howling with laughter. When the last firecracker popped, Grandfather Luong yanked Dad by the arm and escorted him home. On the silent walk, Grandfather pulled a thin knee-high stalk of grassy weed and whipped it against his mischievous son's leg one time. Dad barely felt the sting, but he gazed up and discerned the look of disappointment on his father's face. Dad's heart sank. He felt as though all the bricks in his father's factory had tumbled on top of him. Dad had so much respect for Grandfather Luong that the light whip from a single stalk of grass felt just as intense to him as a fierce, angry blow. Love and respect shown with gentleness can be so much more powerful than force, especially for one prankish boy.

Few things seemed to scare the little boy—except once when, at age six, Dad saw the decapitated head of a man who had been hung from a bamboo tree. On a visit into the countryside to see his grandparents, he and Grandmother Phuong walked toward a crowd gathered around a clump of bamboo shoots. Curious about the ruckus, Grandmother moved closer to take a peek. When she saw the dangling head, she covered Dad's eyes and shielded him behind her. But it was too late; he saw all that was needed to steal his innocence. The crowd of villagers concealed the scene when they swarmed around and pushed him back.

He heard people cursing the "Viet Cong" but did not know what they meant. They said the victim had spoken out against communism. Dad had nightmares for weeks from the sight. He didn't know who the Viet Cong were at that age, but he heard their name again when he saw the remnants of an explosion that blew chunks of cement away from the road. As he got older, the mention of Viet Cong assassinations of villagers and townspeople became regular throughout South Vietnam. The destruction of bridges, roads, and businesses by communist insurgents became the backdrop of his youth.

BY THE TIME DAD entered his teenage years, Grandfather Luong had built a successful brick company that expanded from twenty to one hundred fifty workers and became the primary brick provider for their hometown of Vinh Long and the surrounding villages. Grandfather acquired land and purchased several additional homes in Vinh Long and Saigon. He purchased a new 1968 Peugeot, a rarity for most families in Vietnam. Dad often borrowed the car without permission for joyrides when Grandfather was away.

Life for the children of Dad's generation was not always peaceful or innocent, as the strife between North and South Vietnam escalated after World War II. Vietnam's strategic location in Southeast Asia and its natural resources—the deltas produced a vast supply of exportable rice; the plantations abounded with rubber trees; the mountains were rich in ores—made it a desirable acquisition for foreign invaders, leaving peace and independence a fleeting dream for its people.

Vietnam lost its independence and fell under French imperialist rule starting in 1857 with Napoleon III's decision to invade the country. World War II brought in a new conqueror with the Japanese, who allowed the French to stay only as a figurehead while Japan used Vietnam's

resources to dominate Asia. An underground national independence movement known as the Viet Minh formed in
1941. The rebels and their leader, Ho Chi Minh, organized
clandestine attacks against the French and Japanese with
the goal of purging Vietnam of foreign rulers. The Allied
countries halted Japan's efforts toward world domination
and the Viet Minh expelled the French from Vietnam after
World War II. However, the Viet Minh could not win the
support of all of Vietnam due to its communist leanings
and cruel tactics.

The country was divided ideologically and physically
into North and South. The communist North infiltrated
the pro-democratic South by sending spies and terrorists
with the intent to destroy and prevent progress. Killings
and bombings continually terrorized the people of South
Vietnam. The North wanted to send a message of fear and
intimidation.

An international peace treaty conference held in Geneva,
Switzerland, produced the 1954 Geneva Accords, which
divided Vietnam into North and South at the 17th parallel.
The North would be under the control of the Viet Minh,
led by Ho Chi Minh and backed by Communist China
and the Soviet Union. The South adopted a democratic
state supported by the United States. The Geneva Accords
provided for a temporary division of the country until a
general election in 1956, under the United Nations' supervision, to unite and decide the fate of the country. However,
the election never took place. The North broke the treaty
and steadily attacked and ambushed the South, forcing the
country into a civil war.

As the civil war in Vietnam escalated, a southern counterpart of the Viet Minh emerged, the Viet Cong, wholly
under control of the northern communists. The Viet Cong
were planted into South Vietnam by the North Vietnamese
Army as a guerrilla group to continue the communist

insurgency of terrorism and violence intended to cripple South Vietnam.

To defend the Republic of (South) Vietnam from communist attacks, the Army of the Republic of Vietnam was formed in 1955. The ARVN comprised the ground components that belonged to a larger military organization of South Vietnam called the Republic of Vietnam Armed Forces (RVNAF), which also included the Navy, Marines, Air Force, Regional and Popular Forces, and paramilitaries. The ARVN received financial, material, and personnel support from the United States from 1955 until the US withdrawal in 1973.

DAD STARED AT THE posted result of the 1967 entrance exam for the teaching program in Vinh Long. His name appeared second from the top; three hundred other names followed. He scratched his head and scanned the rest of the list to check for someone with the same name. No mistake; he scored the second highest. Two months earlier, he had graduated from high school and prepared himself for the draft into the military.

South Vietnam's conscription law fated all boys of his generation to military service when they came of age. The same kids who stole fruits with him were now enlisted in the South Vietnamese Army. He wanted to join them. His father, however, ordered him to delay enlistment by entering a two-year teaching program after high school. He reluctantly obeyed and thought a teaching career would be payback for the times he mimicked his teachers, skipped school, and joked in class. A few months later now, in 1968, the Tet Offensive changed everything. As the battles between North and South intensified, the government revoked educational deferments.

VIETNAMESE NEW YEAR'S DAY 1968 exploded with mortar bombs and gunfire instead of fireworks. The North Vietnamese Army (NVA) and Viet Cong insurgents ambushed the South with a massive series of attacks, known as the Tet Offensive, aimed at paralyzing the military and government. "Tet," meaning "festival" in Vietnamese but understood to refer to the New Year celebration, is a national holiday that celebrates the Lunar New Year, which fell on January 30 that year.

In early January 1968, Hanoi announced that it would observe a seven-day ceasefire with the South to celebrate the New Year. The South later learned that the enemy never played fair or by the same rules. While South Vietnam planned for a short break, Hanoi launched approximately 80,000 North Vietnamese soldiers to ambush thirty-six major cities in the South. They attacked US and ARVN bases, airstrips, military headquarters, Saigon police stations, and newspaper buildings. A team of Viet Cong insurgents blew their way into the US Embassy. They held Saigon's radio station captive for six hours before being killed. The communists executed 3,000 civilians in the city of Hue and dumped their bodies in mass graves. They murdered teachers, civil servants, government officials, and citizens who spoke out against communism. The Viet Cong tore the victims from their families. They bound, blindfolded, and shot the victims point-blank or buried them alive. While the North Vietnamese Army fired rockets into southern cities, the Viet Cong threw grenades into schoolyards and bombed churches throughout South Vietnam.

The Viet Cong rained bullets and mortar rounds across cities in the South, which included Dad's hometown, Vinh Long. Bullet holes riddled the smooth walls of historic stone buildings, and shattered glass from blown-out windows spilled into the streets. Frightened citizens hid inside their homes with doors locked and barricaded, while those who could escape fled town, leaving the once bustling streets emptied. In the days following Tet, a knock or a kick on the door heralded Viet Cong searching homes for people who fit the profile to be executed or coerced into their army.

The day after the Tet Offensive, Dad's parents and siblings fled to the brick factory. He stayed behind with Cousin Hung to look after their home. Just out of high school as he was, the Tet Offensive galvanized Dad to join the fight before he had a uniform to put on.

During the battles in and around his city, he settled for a game of cards with Cousin Hung inside their home. The sounds of fists beating at the front door overpowered the noise of cards shuffling. Dad stopped to listen while holding the deck of cards in his hand. The pounding on the door mimicked his heart thumping against his chest. Without hesitation, Dad bolted to the kitchen and pulled out two butcher knives. He handed one to Cousin Hung and said, "I don't want to wear the Viet Cong uniform."

Dad mentally prepared himself to begin the fight that day. The two young men positioned themselves on either side of the door waiting for the Viet Cong to burst inside. Dad fidgeted back and forth and felt the handle of the kitchen knife getting slippery from sweat lathering his palms. The hammering sound seemed like a deafening eternity to Dad but lasted only a few minutes until silence returned. Dad and Hung remained fixed by the door. After an hour, they peeked out the window and saw an empty front yard. Dad still held a firm grip on the butcher knife, refusing to let it go. His cousin had to pry it loose.

GRANDFATHER LUONG DREADED THE thought of having to bury his eldest son. He worried for the fate of his boys, since they were barely young men, and he feared the moment when they reached conscription age. Dad was the first son called to duty.

"Why aren't you eating, *Ba* [father]?" Dad asked Grandfather Luong, who had barely touched the spread of Vietnamese and Chinese food on the dinner table. The aroma of the fresh Vietnamese herbs and Chinese spices, like coriander and ginger, mingled together like Dad's family heritage. The one smell missing from their dinner table that was ubiquitous in every Vietnamese home was *nuoc mam* (fish sauce). Grandfather Luong despised the odor of the decayed condiment and banned it from their kitchen.

Born and raised in Vietnam, Dad considered himself Vietnamese. His father, however, maintained his Chinese identity, despite his high regard for Vietnam. Grandfather Luong immigrated to Vietnam as a young man from southeastern China.

Grandfather kept silent as he moved his chopsticks back and forth in his rice bowl, not picking up any food. He watched his eldest son eat with a hearty appetite and felt full himself, knowing that Dad enjoyed the dinner.

"Son, what do you think about leaving Vietnam and living in Hong Kong until this war ends?"

Dad coughed, almost choking on his food. He resumed eating at a slower pace, trying to digest his father's proposition.

"I have secured travel papers and will finance your life abroad. You must leave before your military report date."

"Can I think about it?" Dad asked. While his eating slowed, his mind raced. He could not decide.

That evening, Dad lay on his bed, staring at his bedroom ceiling, processing the offer that his father had presented. He wrestled over his parents' fear and the real possibility of death and injuries. Yet the powerful urge to join his friends nagged at him. He tossed and turned and played out the different scenarios in his mind until his gut told him what he had to do. He chose to stay and fight.

Dad saw Grandfather Luong's eyes fill with tears on the day he left for boot camp. It pulled at his heart, but he did not want to cause a scene in front of his parents. Dad swung the light bag—that contained only a toothbrush, comb, underwear, and a change of clothes—over his shoulder like a young man without any care. Grandfather pulled him close, tucked some spending money into Dad's pocket, shook his hand, and turned away. Dad waved and said to his parents with youthful confidence, "I'll be fine. I'll make it out safe."

CHAPTER 3

The Cadet

"GET OFF THE TRUCK! Get in line!" the senior classmen hollered to the first batch of cadets entering Thu Duc Military Academy in 1968. Dad grabbed his green duffel bag—packed tight with his issued military uniforms, civilian clothes, metal helmet—and jumped off the military cargo truck alongside the other new soldiers.

"Grab your gear and run!" came the next order. The first group of three hundred men obeyed. With a bag weighing about fifteen pounds on their backs, they ran laps around the academy track, during the searing midday heat, until they completed the three-mile run. Dad played sports in high school but still felt his head throbbing when he neared the finish line. He looked back and saw a few cadets passed out from the heat and the unfamiliar stress on their bodies. The senior classmen, only three months ahead of the new recruits, dragged the collapsed bodies off the track into the shade and gave them water. After several minutes of rest, they plodded back out to complete the run. This was the welcome that each class endured as they entered the accelerated eight-month military program.

South Vietnam had two military schools to train its military officers: the elite Da Lat National Military Academy and the less prestigious but most populated Thu Duc Military Academy. During wartime, the military had to produce graduates to send into battle quick. Wartime cut the four years of training to eight months. The schools cranked out officers insufficiently prepared for battle, which increased the death toll, thus creating its own vicious cycle of supply and demand.

"Get up!" the guard on duty yelled as he entered the barracks at 4 in the morning, waking the slumbering new recruits. Dad, still half asleep, pulled on his white t-shirt and olive-green trousers to start the two-mile run with an M1 Garand rifle on his shoulder. The vintage rifle, an outdated weapon used during WWII and the Korean War, had to suffice for the ARVN forces. Likewise, the issued canvas shoes with their cheap soft rubber soles pinched his feet, but Dad still managed to outrun most of the other cadets. Playing soccer had conditioned him for the runs. A Spartan breakfast of one banana and a piece of bread followed. With not enough time, Dad and his classmates skipped the shower and went straight to the classroom, trailing along their own unique body odor compounded by sweat and dirt. Military lessons lasted until noon. The cadets had fifteen minutes for lunch in the school's canteen to down a meal of rice, stir-fried vegetables, and a small side of fish or pork. Four cadets sat to a table to share the family-style meal.

Dad had a voracious appetite but could not compete with the other hungry trainees. Most of them came from poor families and could eat two bowls of rice even before he could finish his one. They ate up the food before he had his fill.

When the cadets had breaks from their drills, Dad went outside the school to the street markets located steps away from the academy's front entrance with the money that Grandfather Luong regularly sent him. He checked the school meal calendar every week to plan out his lunch schedule. He skipped on days the school canteen served vegetarian meals and headed for food stalls that cooked grilled meat, sizzling over charcoal. He couldn't resist the *nem nuong*, his favorite street food: grilled pork meatballs. He chewed on the meatball skewer while running back to class.

The cadets also relied on home-cooked meals and preserved food their families brought. Nine out of ten recruits came from poor families and ate what the school provided. Dad's closest friends were the poorest guys in his class. He gave them loans using his father's money. He doled out a little cash to his classmates for a beer, a pack of cigarettes, or a meal. Dad considered the small loan a morale booster. By graduation, his friends had amassed a huge debt, which he never collected.

After lunch, classroom lessons took up the rest of the day and stretched to 9 in the evening. Dad returned to his barrack and flopped onto his bed. In a few hours, the men would have to get up again for the morning run and repeat the day.

The makeshift barrack with sheet metal roof and walls had gaps that welcomed dust and the outside elements in. It was a constant chore to keep the dust down. The senior classman ran his gloved fingers along the rail of Dad's lower bunk bed during a barrack inspection. He ordered Dad, "Give me twenty push-ups. Your bed has dirt on it." He continued, "Give me another twenty; your shoes are dusty." Then he opened the small locker where Dad stored his clothes and found more dust, adding on another twenty push-ups. By the end of the daily inspection, Dad had accumulated over sixty push-ups, which he did in successive bursts. It was the third month into training, and by that

Dad reads a letter from home during a break at Thu Duc Military Academy in 1968. (Courtesy of Tran B. Quan)

point, Dad was fit. He jumped up after knocking out the push-ups with a grin on his flushed red face, then took out a rag and wiped his bed and locker.

One day a week, the cadets received their rest and relaxation. Dad's friends once found him sitting at a canteen table absorbed in reading a letter from home. They peeked over his shoulder to look at the letter and noted the handwriting of a girl who signed her name Gia. A photo of a girl with delicate porcelain skin and a cascade of glossy black hair that went to her waist slipped from the pages. Dad thought Mom was the prettiest girl in Vinh Long—or in any town, as far as he was concerned.

At age twenty, he didn't have many solid plans, except for these two: to marry Mom and to join the battle. Of course, the closer to graduation Dad got, the more worried Grandfather Luong became.

Grandfather stuffed money into Dad's pockets on visits, even when Dad halfheartedly declined. Grandmother

Phuong protested, "You'll spoil him." But Grandfather didn't listen. He feared his eldest son's life might be cut short at any time and a little spending wouldn't do any harm.

Dad stood at his post with two recruits one evening during guard duty, looking in the direction of the garrison movie theater. He had a few dollars in his pocket for movie tickets that quiet evening. He debated in his head the best course to follow.

"Let's go have some fun," he finally decided. The other two cadets joined him. They hid their weapons and headed for the theater. While watching Dad's favorite actor, John Wayne, land on a Normandy beach in *The Longest Day*, they heard two loud booms!

"That's not from the movie," Dad told his buddies. "Let's go!" They sprinted back to their post, grabbed their weapons, and ran toward the defense line along with the rest of the recruits. They positioned themselves behind a four-foot mud wall that encircled the academy, with weapons aimed. After firing only two mortar rounds into the compound, the enemy ran off. The cadets returned to their post when the commanding officer gave the all-clear. Later, they discovered that one mortar blast had taken the life of a student.

Mortar attacks on the school by the Viet Cong became a common occurrence, as did attacks outside the school on unsuspecting civilians.

After only eight months of training, Dad and a drove of recruits crowded around the posted list for class rank, a week before graduation. Dad started from the bottom of the list and worked his way up. Once again, he did not expect to find his name near the top. "You are number 15 out of 720!" his friend exclaimed with disbelief.

The cadets contested for safe assignments like those at the National Training Center, one of the largest military training centers for enlisted soldiers in South Vietnam. The top graduates got the first pick of duties, and the desirable spots filled first. The units that saw the heaviest fighting went to those graduating at the bottom of the class.

Dad's parents urged him to take a safe position at the training center which his class rank allowed. He chose instead to join ARVN's 9th Infantry Division, known for its heavy combat missions and for its commander, Tran Ba Di.

CHAPTER 4

The First Imprisonment

THE SUN GLEAMED OVER the clear blue Florida sky, the warm summer air mingled with the gulf breeze, and the automobile odyssey continued toward Key West. "How are you holding up, General?" Dad asked, patting his division commander on the knee. "There's a nice park in Sarasota up ahead. Do you want to make a stop?" Dad itched for Cousin Hung to pull over for a break, so that he could have a cigarette.

General Di replied with a chuckle, "Do not worry about me, Younger Brother. But if you want to make a stop, I would not mind stretching my legs."

From Orlando to Sarasota, General Di never uttered a request or complaint. He sat contentedly with his eyes focused on the road, observing the street signs. Occasionally, he took out a worn notebook that seemed like a weathered travel companion and jotted down an English word he saw on a billboard or heard in conversation that interested him. Later, he looked up the word or phrase and laughed at the cleverness or silliness of his discovery.

We pulled into a park along the coastline. Everyone got out and walked toward the restroom. Dad helped General Di out and stayed by the car to finish his cigarette.

"Do not smoke so much or I will tell your wife!" General Di teased.

We gathered outside the restroom then walked together toward the glimmering water to soak in the sun. Cousin Hung rummaged in the back of the van for water. He approached the group, carrying a red cooler. Inside were eight fresh green coconuts with their tops chopped open. Cousin Hung gave everyone a straw with their coconut. A cool sea breeze blew in while we drank coconut juice. No one wanted to say anything to disturb the moment.

That is, until Dad said, "Wish I had a beer right now!" Mom glared at Dad. General Di burst into a laugh, and everyone joined in.

"The sky, water, and coconut remind me a little of my hometown," General Di said.

I asked, "Sir, what was your childhood in Vietnam like?"

"It was a good childhood," General Di gave his measured answer.

"Were you affected by the upheaval of the time?" I persisted, wanting to know more. Learning about Dad's youth and the strife of that period gave me a better understanding of his past. But I still wondered how my father's generation coped with war, especially one fought right at their doorstep.

Sensing my genuine curiosity and seeing the inquisitive looks from the other passengers, General Di began, "At the age of fourteen, I was jailed." The general slowly pulled from his memory the childhood that was affected by the turbulent political climate even before the Vietnam War started.

Sarasota sunset at a Florida rest area. From left to right: Dad, Dad's friend Thanh Du, General Di, Mom, Cousin Hung, and Hung's wife Hoang. (Courtesy of Tran B. Quan)

IN 1945, DI BECAME a political prisoner with his father and uncle when the French troops swept the Vietnamese countryside for suspected dissidents. His family, along with thousands of others in provinces across Vietnam, participated in a scorched earth tactic that advocated the burning and destruction of personal property such as crops and homes so that the opposing enemy could not confiscate and make use of the assets. They protested the return of French occupation in Vietnam after World War II.

Di's father joined the protest against French rule. He torched his family's home and fled with them to the countryside. Others in their hometown did the same and left the town abandoned in ashes. They wanted their independence and the French out of their country. French troops responded with mass arrests, attempting to extinguish the revolt.

When Di, his father, and his uncle were captured and imprisoned, his mother, Tran Thi Thanh, a petite woman with a pleasant round face and hair pulled back in a sensible bun, ran to the home of an acquaintance she knew who was friendly with the French forces. She prayed his influence could rescue the men of her family. She banged on the door with frantic hands until the man opened it. She pleaded with him to come to the prison with her.

A fourteen-year-old Di sat on the dirt floor, crammed together with two hundred other political detainees in a building within a prison complex built by the French. A small box in the corner of the dark dungeon served as a toilet. The prison guard threw one small loaf of hard, stale bread at him that had to last for the day along with a cup of murky water. The squalor and stench extinguished his hunger.

His uncle, sitting beside him, urged him to eat. Di took a small bite of the bread and forced it down with water that had an aftertaste of mud. He couldn't finish the rest. His thoughts kept returning to his father, whom the guards had separated from the group after a few questions on the first day in prison. That had been two days ago. Di witnessed other men whisked away from the mass and thrown back into the building with swollen lips and faces with purple bruises. Even at a young age, he noted the stoic dignity of the beaten prisoners. He wondered if his father had met the same fate. His stomach churned with fear and worry.

Di closed his eyes and buried his head into his folded arms. He drifted off to sleep only to be awakened minutes later by the shake on his arm from his uncle. The guards unshackled the chains and led Di and his uncle out to the prison courtyard, where his mother waited.

"Where is Father?" Di asked.

"They are still questioning him," she said with a strained look. The French interrogators assumed that an educated man like Di's father, Tran Van Vang—the head counselor at Nguyen Dinh Chieu, the largest high school in South Vietnam in 1945—would have a role in the uprising.

In a dim, musty room, a few kerosene lamps threw their light on the two opposing sides. The French interrogators leaned across the table toward the Vietnamese man with a patrician face and detached stare. The interrogators pushed for answers, but Tran Van Vang repeated his truth. He had torched his home with his own free will. He was not affiliated with any resistance group.

They grabbed Tran Van Vang by the collar, led him to a room with a sink, and tied his arm behind his back. While one interrogator wrapped a cloth around his face, another turned the faucet on to let out a gradual stream of water. Tran Van Vang felt a tug on his hair, then a slow stream of water on his face that saturated the towel. The unceasing flow of water made him feel suffocated. He couldn't breathe through the heavy wet towel. He felt like he was drowning in a deep sea.

Still, Tran Van Vang stood firm. After ten days without getting any information from him, the French decided that he did not have political ties to the growing Viet Minh movement, whose mission at that time was to overthrow French sovereignty in Vietnam. Tran Van Vang returned home to his family, beaten and gaunt but not defeated. From his torture, he tried to impart a life lesson to his eldest son—rooted not from hate but from humanity.

"Treat every human being with compassion, even your enemy." Tran Van Vang used a tale about a dying Moor soldier to instruct his son after his release from prison. The story tells of a French general fighting the Moors in the Islamic empire 1,300 years ago who witnessed a Moor soldier nearing death. The soldier begged for a drink of water. The general's aide did not want to offer the enemy any water. But the French general said, "Give him a drink. Treat him as a human being." His father's lessons and the story stayed with Di throughout his life.

Aside from his first political imprisonment, Di experienced a relatively calm youth. Born on July 20, 1931, in the city of My Tho, Di was destined to lead from the start, being the oldest of eleven children. His platoon of siblings followed their gentle brother's lead. He never bossed or fought with them. Instead, his influence led all three younger brothers to join him in military service.

As a boy growing up in My Tho, Di swam in the rivers of his hometown and roamed the countryside with his friends. He was not the strongest swimmer or the fastest runner, but that didn't stop him from competing with the best of them. Sometimes, after a run, when he felt his chest tighten and he knew that the wheezing and coughing fits would soon follow, he'd find a quiet place away from the stares of others to collect himself. His friends did not know that he had flares of asthma that left him struggling to breathe. He relied on home remedies his mother brewed from herbs and roots used in traditional folk medicine. He would not let asthma affect his love of the outdoors or limit his participation in sports. Eventually, he outgrew the childhood asthma and maintained robust health during his young adulthood.

Most Vietnamese of Di's generation, especially those from the countryside villages, did not further their education beyond elementary school. The sacrifices compelled of poor families and the rigorous academic requirements modeled after the French school system made obtaining a high school diploma difficult.

Di modestly described himself as an "average" student. Yet, those who enrolled in Vietnam's school system during that period knew that an average student would not have advanced in the time or with the ease that Di demonstrated. His character indicated a student who was cerebral and earnest.

Di completed his secondary education at the Collège Le Myre de Villers in My Tho from 1944 to 1949. He then studied at the Lycée Chasseloup-Laubat in Saigon from 1949 to 1951. Consequently, he learned to write and speak fluent French.

Di's time at the *lycée* followed a steady path toward a teaching career like that of his father until a fateful speech given at the school's graduation ceremony changed the course of his life. General Jean Joseph Marie Gabriel de Lattre de Tassigny, a decorated French military hero and high commissioner and commander in chief of French forces in Indochina, stepped to the podium and delivered a discourse calling for young Vietnamese men to join the newly formed Vietnamese Army to help Vietnam move closer to independence and eliminate communist resistance.

De Lattre exclaimed, "Be men! . . . If you are patriots, fight for your country, because this war is yours!" Di sat in the audience, spellbound by the French general's passionate speech.

At nineteen, Di wanted to join the cause for an independent Vietnam but not through the murderous tactics used by the communist Viet Minh. He shared the hope of many Vietnamese for French rule in Vietnam to end. At the same time, he recognized the growing dangers of communism in Vietnam as it gained momentum from China and into Southeast Asia.

CHAPTER 5

The Young Officer

FOR TWO DAYS IN 1951, Di sat through rounds of written examinations with over two thousand applicants vying for a spot in the prestigious Da Lat National Military Academy. The school sought to produce an "elite" professional officer corps, with roughly one out of ten applicants making the selection. To be considered, applicants had to be between the ages of eighteen and twenty-two, be unmarried, and have completed high school. After a thorough physical exam and a series of rigorous academic tests, Di found himself among the 250 cadets selected for the class of 1952.

He travelled over 200 miles north from the lowland of his hometown to the city of Da Lat, located in the Central Highlands region of Vietnam. Along the way, he discovered a part of Vietnam much different from the landscape he had known. He passed through French rubber and tea plantations planted on rolling hills. Further north, he climbed over the steep Prenn Pass, where he gazed out to see a chain of mountains covered with majestic pine trees. The cool, light air of the highland region complemented the clean pine scent.

Perched on a hill five kilometers north of the city center, overlooking Lac des Soupirs (Lake of Sighs), Da Lat National Military Academy waited. In its early days, the minimalistic compound consisted of wooden barracks, a cadet mess hall, a gymnasium, a recreation center, and office buildings. In 1959, President Ngo Diem expanded the school, transforming it into a modern four-year military academy known as the "West Point of South Vietnam."

Di's mastery of the French language made the culture and atmosphere of the French military academy familiar. However, he had to pass through the newly established tradition of "metamorphosis" in the first month in which cadets were expected to transform overnight into disciplined soldiers. They endured an initial period of intense mental and physical hazing to hone them into soldiers who could uphold the French military code of conduct: "obey without hesitation nor murmur."

The new recruits found respite during the free weekends in the resort atmosphere of Da Lat, where they could enjoy the city's fine French restaurants and hotels, surrounded by the breathtaking natural beauty of waterfalls, lakes, and forests. The quaint stone homes and shops of Da Lat, with red roofs set against a backdrop of mountains and hills covered with green fir trees, reminded Di of a town somewhere in the French Alps that he'd seen in magazines. But his heart remained true to the palms and rice paddies of the Mekong Delta and his hometown sweetheart.

Di progressed through his courses without difficulty and graduated eight months later, on May 1, 1952, to join the newly formed Vietnam National Army (VNA). The VNA later transitioned into the ARVN with guidance from the United States.

At twenty-one, Di became a platoon leader in the South Vietnamese Army's Sixty-First Infantry Battalion in the rural district of Duc Hoa in 1952. Second Lieutenant Di took charge of thirty soldiers assigned to secure the roads for civilian travel. At night, the communist insurgents, later organized into the Viet Cong, came out to destroy the roads. With sharp picks and axes, they dug wide and deep holes or piled mounds of dirt across the road, making travel and daily life difficult for the local citizens. Around this time, the insurgents started planting land mines, a practice that escalated in later years of the war. They would often get village sympathizers to help them carry out the sabotage.

After six months as a platoon leader, Di received new orders returning him to Da Lat Military Academy to train new cadets. He spent eight months as an instructor, teaching weaponry, map reading, and military tactics. He liked teaching, but the draw of a fighting unit pulled at him. He requested to be assigned to a combat unit.

From 1952 to 1954, Di carried on his military duties amidst the backdrop of momentous transitions in Vietnam's history. France retreated from Vietnam after its loss to the Viet Minh in the Battle of Dien Bien Phu in 1954. The surrender meant the end of French imperialism in Vietnam. But the country remained ideologically divided, with the communist-backed North opposing a Republic South.

In 1956, Di was promoted to the rank of captain. He served in the 582nd Battalion, 134th Territorial Regiment, which was part of the Regional Forces located in the Delta region of South Vietnam. He commanded a battalion of approximately four hundred militiamen soldiers. The South Vietnamese Army recruited them from villages and provinces and assigned them to defend their local bridges, ferries, and towns. They were considered the poor cousin to the regular army. Consequently, they received the worst equipment, consisting of vintage weapons left by the French from the World War II era. Low on weapons and burdened with inadequately trained manpower, Di learned early the struggles of the Vietnamese fighting force.

Di tried to build the morale of these often-marginalized soldiers by finding opportunities to recognize them. In turn, the militiamen wanted to do a good job for him and stood taller when they wore what little issued gear he could give them over their farmer's garb. The village militiamen proved to be more skillful and vital than they were per-ceived by the established military community. They had firsthand knowledge of the ins and outs of the local area and knew the jungle like their backyard. Under the right influence, the citizen-soldiers became an asset.

When their bravery and actions merited reward, Di rec-ognized them like professional soldiers. The shoeless village militiamen stood straight at attention and beamed as the young captain pinned army medals on their sun-bleached shirts. Word soon spread through the region about the young army officer. Thus began the establishment of Tran Ba Di's reputation and his winning of the "hearts and minds" of the people of the Mekong Delta.

"GOOD MORNING!" THE VIETNAMESE teacher in the Saigon classroom spoke the words in a slow, exaggerated English to the thirty South Vietnamese officers. Di sat in the private language class with his fellow officers, getting a crash course in English before the group's trip to America. The military selected their top officers to repre-sent South Vietnam in a joint training with their American counterpart in the Infantry Advanced Course at Fort

Major Di awards a medal to a village militiaman in 1963. (Courtesy of Harry McFarland)

Benning, Georgia, in 1957.* Both countries could foresee a long and necessary partnership as US involvement in Vietnam deepened.

On the plane ride to the US, Di looked out the window into the blueness of the Pacific Ocean with the wonderment of a young man on an adventure. The trip marked his first time on an airplane and travel outside the country, both unimaginable experiences for most Vietnamese in 1957. Their plane landed at Fairfield, California's Travis Air Force Base. The abundance and modernity of America immediately struck Di with awe. His eyes fixed on the paved roads that sustained more cars than he had ever seen at one time. The office buildings and stores looked at least twice the size of the buildings left from the French colonial days in the best quarters of Saigon.

From California, the officers traveled by rail to Fort Benning. Di admired the natural beauty of America's rolling golden hills and mountain ranges. They passed through small farming towns and saw cattle grazing on the open range. Looking out the train window as the mighty steam engine chugged along the track, Di thought to himself that America was blessed with more natural and industrial richness than he and his countrymen had ever seen.

When the group arrived at Fort Benning, Di saw an Army band on the field. He wondered about its presence there and why a crowd had gathered. Then he heard the band playing South Vietnam's national anthem, followed by "The Star-Spangled Banner," and he understood. Fort Benning had prepared a welcoming ceremony for the South Vietnamese officers. Di watched the American and Vietnamese flags waving together against the Georgia sky. He stood taller believing that the US considered his

* The Advanced Course was designed to augment the leadership skills of the army officer in areas of troop-leading procedures, battlefield intelligence preparation, reconnaissance, and military decision-making.

countrymen allies—a stark contrast to the years under French rule where Vietnamese were viewed as subjects.

After training at Fort Benning, Di travelled to Camp Pendleton, California, for a two-month course in amphibious operations. In San Diego, he participated in a combined operation working with the US Army, Navy, and Marines. Those were happy times for him, especially Fridays, when the chow hall served "all of the good food" that he could eat. Once, on a weekend pass, his fellow American officers took him on a day trip to Tijuana, Mexico. The experience for Di was not the same as for the other soldiers; he didn't drink, smoke, or join in the rowdiness. But when asked about his time in Tijuana, without going into detail he'd give a sly smile and say, "It was fun."

Some years later, in 1965, Di returned to the United States to attend the US Army Command and General Staff College at Fort Leavenworth, Kansas. Afterward, Di headed to Fort Bragg, North Carolina, for a six-month course in counterinsurgency and psychological warfare. Even while appreciating the abundant US military training and knowledge he gained, Di knew that he could not realistically apply all of it to a poorly equipped South Vietnamese army, despite American support.

CHAPTER 6
The Mission

ON THAT MIDDAY IN June, the coconut drinks that Cousin Hung provided at the Sarasota park quenched our thirst, but the beverage was not enough to appease our bellies. Still within the town of Sarasota on our road trip, we stopped at a Chinese buffet restaurant for lunch. We found a table large enough to fit all eight of us. I watched our belongings while everyone wandered around the array of food making their selections. Sitting alone, I reflected on the tales of Dad's wayward youth in contrast to General Di's earnest past. They were so different, yet there they were walking back to the table and sitting side by side like kindred souls.

Dad looked down at his plate, piled high with food, and said, "We didn't eat like this during the war."

"What did you eat?" I asked,

"Snakes, rodents—whatever we could catch on the trails during our missions. Just as long as it wasn't bullets." Dad winked.

"The poor soldiers," General Di said in a somber voice.

Dads looks out on the grounds of the ARVN unit in 1970. (Courtesy of Tran B. Quan)

"What was it like fighting in the war?" I wanted to know. Dad never talked much about it, so I never knew how it affected him. When the subject was mentioned, an impish glint appeared in his eyes, chased away by a forlorn sigh.

Both men gave me ambivalent looks. I had, unknowingly, pulled out opposing memories of love, hate, brotherhood, and loss. They said nothing for a few seconds, then Dad broke the silence and uttered, "There are some things too hard to describe. But I will try."

DAD ARRIVED AT HIS first assignment as a platoon leader with the ARVN's 9th Infantry Division, 15th Regiment, after graduation from Thu Duc Academy in April 1969. Before he could unload his gear, the unit sent his platoon out on an operation. Since the division became a mobile unit that year it meant that the troops were constantly moving. Dad barely returned to regimental headquarters in Sa Dec. The missions required him and his platoon to be on the move for twenty-eight days straight with two days off.

On one such operation, the point man, barely out of his teenage years, signaled with one arm halfway raised and fist clenched, warning Dad and his platoon of twenty-five soldiers several hundred yards behind to stop. Danger lay ahead. Dad ordered his troops to take a knee on the dirt path. He pulled out his Colt .45 pistol while his soldiers had their rifles in hand. Seconds later, they heard popping gunfire from AK-47s in the distance. They took cover behind bushes and palm trees and shot in the direction of enemy fire. After several minutes of no return fire, they regrouped and continued their patrol along a dirt path flanked on both sides with green rice paddies. Dad figured the Viet Cong had retreated. Like their American counterparts, the ARVN troops found the enemy elusive. In a blink, the Viet Cong melted into the jungle or blended in with the locals. The Viet Cong were Vietnamese, like them, and dressed in village clothes like the people they set out to protect. Dad radioed headquarters to report the encounter.

Dad looked down at his watch; it was almost noon. At five that morning, before the village roosters crowed, he and his platoon had set out to reach the destination point that headquarters had ordered them to cover that day. They were sent on a search-and-destroy mission to find Viet Cong insurgents along the Mekong Delta. The regiment's colonel gave orders only hours before they headed out on foot for fear of information leaks into enemy hands. The operation changed from day to day, depending on the enemy's tactics.

Dad and his men walked for another hour before taking a short break. The afternoon sun, high and merciless, blazed down on them. They found shade in a cluster of banana trees and conducted a quick visual survey of the surrounding rice paddies before settling down. Several hundred feet away, Dad noted a few farmers squatting in the rice field with straw hats watching their water buffalos graze nearby. His glance darted back to them every few minutes, never sure whom he could trust. While his soldiers took out their water canteens, Dad reached for his belt pack with his map, a pencil, and a few pieces of candy inside. He pulled out his compass from a small pouch attached to his pistol belt and noted their location on the map. Two more miles left before they reached their destination for the day.

"You have any cigarettes, Lieutenant?" a soldier asked.

Dad pulled out a half-emptied pack and offered it to the soldier and a few others who were craving a smoke. The sensation of nicotine temporarily numbed their fears and fueled their wearied bodies. A few minutes later, Dad popped a piece of candy in his mouth, checked the two grenades attached to both sides of his chest to make sure they were secured to his suspenders, and ordered his troops back on the trail.

They continued along the dirt path. A gust of wind blew ripples through the blooming green rice paddies of late spring. Dad caught a whiff of light fragrance from the flowering stalks of rice as a breeze blew by. The warm aroma reminded him of rice cooking at home, but lighter and with a floral hint. The towering clusters of palm and coconut trees swayed back and forth together like they were dancing in the wind. For a moment, he forgot about the stench of blood, body odor, and gunpowder. He noted a few straw-roof homes with a handful of chickens scratching the ground outside. His gaze paused at a pair of clotheslines hanging in front of homes where children's garments flapped in the wind. It reminded him of a normal life. The deceptively serene countryside pulled him into its charm. He had become accustomed to the unpredictable days that oscillated between violence and peace.

The group reached a stopping point at dusk near the outskirts of a village. They had covered five miles that day, from dawn to dusk. The platoon made camp for the night near a village house. After a few minutes of rest, Dad divided the squads into separate areas to camp in case of an ambush. He scanned the area, looking for clusters of trees or any structures that would shield his soldiers. Once the squads scattered into their respective areas, each soldier dug a foxhole, three feet wide and three feet deep, to jump in if they came under attack. Of the nine soldiers in each squad, three took turns throughout the night to guard.

After the platoon sergeant inspected the foxholes, the soldiers ate. They took out their small pots, filled them with dry rice and water, and cooked them over a fire. A few men carried parcels of dried meat to eat with their rice, but most ate whatever they caught or foraged on the trail. When the soldiers stopped for breaks, they scoured the area for moving critters like frogs, snakes, and turtles. Other times, Dad saw some of his soldiers eat rice with just salt mixed with chili peppers. Each month the soldiers received a small stipend to purchase food for field operations. The regiment supplied the rice, but additional food had to be purchased. The soldiers earned less than thirty dollars a month. With hungry families to support, they sent the extra money home and went without.

THREE WEEKS INTO THE operation and only a few miles away from the next destination point of another day, the point man gave a signal and the platoon stopped. A thin nylon line almost invisible to most eyes poked through a dried clump of cracked dirt along the path. "Land mine!" the point man yelled back.

It was the beginning of the monsoon season that May 1969, which meant that land mines would soon become harder to spot. The unrelenting rain would pour straight down to dampen the dried clumps along dirt roads and make the countryside foliage green and lush, while hiding the land mines and trip wires. When the monsoon season came—and it lasted six months, from May through October—even the best point man could be distracted by the rain and mud. But Dad's platoon got lucky when the sun lingered one last day to keep the dirt path baked and cracked.

"Blow it up," Dad said to his platoon sergeant. Everyone moved back. A soldier aimed his rifle and fired at the target until it exploded, sending a shower of clumped dirt with black smoke in the air. Dad exhaled a sigh of relief: one more disaster averted.

The experienced platoon sergeants selected a handful of quick and clever young soldiers with sharp vision, gave them several months of training for scout work, then sent them in front of the platoon or company during missions. They scanned the surroundings for hazards like grenades hanging from trees, jungle booby traps, and land mines. Dad's point men could detect the thinnest trip wires.

Toward evening of that day, the platoon settled in the dirt yard of a village home. Dad dropped his gear in a corner of the yard next to his friend Second Lieutenant Tri (a supply officer) and his platoon sergeant. The dirt floor would be their bed, and the leaves of the banana tree their cover. They were about to cook their rice when the homeowner, a village man with a long wispy white beard and teeth stained black from chewing betel nut, approached them with an offer. "Would you men like to come inside my house to share a meal? I do not have much, just a few simple dishes."

The three stood up and followed the man inside his home while the rest of the platoon tended to their campfire meal. A bowl of boiled squash and a plate of fried perch sat on the table. The old man poured them some of his home-brewed liquor. They raised their cups and accepted the villager's generosity but remained cautious. They could not be sure of whom to trust in the remote countryside, where the Viet Cong had infiltrated and built a strong following.

The village man asked Dad, "Young man, may I read your palm? It is a skill passed down in my family." Dad hesitated; he did not believe in fortune-telling. But he didn't see any harm and showed the man his palm.

"By age thirty-one, you will no longer live in Vietnam," the villager predicted. Dad did not want to think or ask about what he meant. He thanked the man and returned to his camp outside. He took out his poncho and spread it on the ground. Before he lay down for the night, Dad pulled out his map and pencil to review their progress. They had more land to cover before they could circle back to head-quarters. He folded his map and tucked it back into his pouch.

Dad closed his eyes and tried to sleep, but even the symphony of croaking frogs, hooting owls, and buzzing mosquitoes could not drown out the snore of his friend, Tri. When the snoring got louder, Dad gave Tri a swift kick in the leg. Five minutes later, the snoring returned. Dad grumbled, took his poncho, and moved to another corner in the yard. He wondered how a small guy like Tri, who barely topped five feet and who weighed around 120 pounds, could be that loud. Tri could sleep under any conditions. Every break they took, he napped.

The light sprinkle of misty rain on his face woke Dad the next morning and ushered in the dreaded monsoon rain. The sun hid behind low dark clouds saturated with water droplets. After he washed his face with water from his canteen and drank the rest, he headed out with the troops. Sweat clung to his body and the sticky humidity trapped heat. The damp air made breathing difficult, especially with the weight of his gear. By midmorning, the rain came down harder, like liquid pellets, but he and his troops pushed on. The pull of mud on his boots slowed his steps. Water soaked the fabric cover on the top of Dad's boots, and his rubber soles threatened to split. He scratched the hard bumps of mosquito bites on his neck and swatted a live one away from his face.

Dad's platoon encountered more water when they approached a swamp that led into a jungle. He entered the chest-high water holding up his gun and pouch with map and compass above his head, while his soldiers held their rifles with both hands in the air. Rain poured down. It rinsed the muddy water from their clothes when they made their way out of the swamp.

Dad spotted a small black lump attached to his arm. "You've got a leech on you, Lieutenant. I'll get it out for you," a soldier offered. The soldier took out a bit of salt and sprinkled it over the leech. The leech released its hold. Dad flung it into the mud.

After they crossed the swamp, a dense jungle abundant with mangrove trees and different species of palms waited for them. The mangrove tree resembles a broom, with a thin trunk and a bottom that flares out with a mesh of twig-like branches. Tri joked with Dad, "You think these trees make good coffins?"

"Keep your eyes open and watch your step," Dad reminded his troops. The canopy of trees covered whatever little light the morning gave. The platoon kept watch for scattered booby traps across the jungle paths.

The platoon sergeant called to Dad, "Lieutenant, the soldiers found something." They uncovered a pit, four feet deep with rows of sharpened bamboo spears sticking up from the ground inside. A stick frame over the pit, covered with leaves, concealed the trap. The hole could swallow and impale at least two soldiers. They saw the death trap clearer when the morning clouds broke apart and allowed a burst of light to flash through the foliage.

Dad ordered the soldiers to pull out the bamboo spikes and neutralize the trap. They smashed the stick frame and uncovered the pit. The platoon sergeant tied a strip of cloth to a stake and stuck it by the pit to warn other troops.

By late afternoon, they found an opening out of the jungle. The dead vegetation cleared a path for them. "Don't touch any plants or your skin will blister. It looks like Agent Orange," the platoon sergeant warned.*

One evening, on the last week of the mission, the platoon made its way to an empty village school. The troops decided to borrow a classroom and take shelter for the night before the students returned in the morning. Tri pulled two desks together and fell asleep on the top before the sun sank. Dad couldn't sleep yet, and he could not resist a prank while watching Tri snore away. He took a string and gently tied it around Tri's two big toes. Then he wadded a small piece of paper from a student's desk and squeezed it into a tight roll. He inserted the paper roll in between Tri's tied toes. Dad took out his lighter and lit the small roll of paper on fire. Tri woke from the sear of flame against his skin and saw the fire at his feet. He spun off the desks and fell to the ground. Dad let out a loud roar of laughter. Tri reached for his pistol, and Dad darted out the door. Tri chased after the prankster but could not catch him. Dad retreated to his hiding place for the rest of the night. The next morning, when they met up, Dad gave his friend an unremorseful smile. Tri shoved Dad's shoulder and smiled back. They left the school before the students arrived.

---

* The US military sprayed the herbicide Agent Orange over the jungles and fields of Vietnam to destroy the thick vegetation, obliterating the Viet Cong's jungle hideouts and clearing land for ARVN and US troop movement. The toxic defoliant destroyed targeted vegetation but also damaged the health of those who came into contact with it.

By the end of the fourth week, the platoon returned home to the 15th Regimental Headquarters without taking any losses. However, a few soldiers had infected bites from spiders, wasps, ants, scorpions, and a host of jungle insects. Some had macerated skin coming off their feet from walking days with socks soaked from rain and swamp water.

The leech bite on Dad's arm turned into a warm red mound with pus seeping out. The regiment did not have enough medics to go out on operations. Unless suffering from life-threatening emergencies, soldiers waited for treatment until they returned to the garrison. They headed to the regimental clinic where Dr. Khuc Hieu Duc saw patients from morning to late afternoon without taking any breaks.

CHAPTER 7

Respite

DAD STOOD AT THE doorway of the regimental clinic with a group of soldiers. He touched the warm red mass on his forearm then picked at the scab that formed over the pustular head. The soldiers around him squirmed and paced, some holding their bellies from the adverse effects of food scavenged on the trails while a few others shivered with sweat beaded on their foreheads from malaria. The medic told them to wait and allow Dr. Duc to have a quick break.

"Do not make them wait. I can see them now," Dr. Duc said in a low, mild voice. A stocky man with spectacles, the thirty-year-old regimental physician had been commissioned into the military straight out of medical school.

Earlier that morning, Dr. Duc had finished a house call visit, treating a soldier's family who lived near headquarters. He stayed with the family from the late-night hours until dawn, then went to examine patients already waiting for him in morning clinic.

He said little as he cleaned Dad's infection with alcohol and squeezed out the remaining pus until the abscess flattened. The doctor listened and gave an empathetic nod as Dad told him about the mission his platoon had completed. He handed Dad a small plastic bag with antibiotics and instructed him to follow up the next day. Dr. Duc took his break only after the last soldiers received treatment.

Dad went to see Dr. Duc the next day as instructed. His infection had improved, and he wanted to thank the doctor. "Come join us for a beer, Doc," Dad invited. Dr. Duc obliged and hopped into the jeep with Dad and three of his friends later that evening.

They headed into town to their hangout spot, an outdoor food stall that sold cheap beer. A row of similar food stalls lined the boulevard that accommodated businesses and homes built in the French colonial style. Knee-high tables with foot stools provided customers a front-row view of the street market bustle. From the table, they could see and hear the traffic a few feet way. The honking French Citroën cars, roaring motorbikes, bicycles with ringing bells, and chatter of people weaving through the street mingled together like a chaotic symphony. Around them merchants hawked local fruits, meats, and clothing. Walking vendors carried baskets filled with mangos, boiled peanuts, and homemade rice cakes wrapped in banana leaves. Pedestrians, vendors, and motorists moved in unison like a feverish choreographed dance. From their table, Dad and his friends sometimes caught the sight of girls on bicycles wearing silk *ao dai*: a traditional ankle-length garment with waist-high slit worn with matching flowing silk pants. The ends of the white and pastel dresses fluttered by like exotic butterflies. The simple enchantment of the scene gave the observers' minds a mental break from the mayhem of war.

The day's heat and the exhaust fumes from the street made them thirsty. Dad ordered a round of 33 Beer, a

French beer cheap enough for him to treat everyone. Dr. Duc was still sipping on his first bottle when the guys were on their fifth and sixth. The doctor's face flushed from less than half a twelve-ounce bottle.

"Finish it, Doc!" Dad and his friends hollered.

They egged him on to drink more, but he smiled and shook his head. The following week, Dr. Duc joined them again; this time, they spurred him to chug two bottles of beer. When they returned from the field a month later, he finished four bottles of beer without any prompting. By the end of the third month, Dr. Duc could outdrink everyone at the table, even those twice his size. His drinking buddies looked at him with a new respect. Dr. Duc even helped carry Dad back to the jeep when he passed out trying to keep up with the doctor. Fortunately for the regiment, Dr. Duc remained dedicated to his profession despite his new hobby.

Dad did not have the same fondness for all army doctors that he did for Dr. Duc. When Dad transferred to the 16th Regiment, in 1970, he encountered a doctor the soldiers secretly named "Dr. Rotten Tomato." This doctor did not have the same dedication as Dr. Duc. Instead of tending to the sick and wounded, Dr. Rotten Tomato kept a strict schedule for his afternoon naps. Near noontime, he retreated to his bunker, changed into his silk pajamas and slippers, and napped for two hours. He gave orders to his medics not to disturb him. The soldiers knew his rituals well—but not Dad, whose new responsibility involved evacuating wounded troops back to the rear.

During a day of heavy casualties, Dad brought back dozens of soldiers exposed to Agent Orange. They limped into the regimental aid station with hands and feet covered with blisters and ruptured weeping sores. He looked for Dr. Rotten Tomato, but the medics told him that the doctor had retired for his afternoon rest. Dad stormed to the doctor's quarters and pounded on the door.

From behind the door, Dr. Rotten Tomato shouted, "What do you want? Didn't I give orders not to disturb me at this time?"

Dad returned, "This is Lieutenant Le Quan. I have injured soldiers that need to be seen now!"

Rotten Tomato replied, "Go away. I will see them when I am ready."

Dad left and headed straight to the office of his regimental commander, Colonel Nguyen Van Hai, and briefly explained the situation. Without saying a word, the colonel calmly put on his cap and jacket and walked with Dad to Dr. Rotten Tomato's bunker.

Colonel Hai knocked on the door. Rotten Tomato answered impatiently, "What do you want now? Didn't I tell you to go away?"

Colonel Hai politely answered with a controlled voice hinting at outrage and sarcasm, "This is Colonel Hai, doctor. My men are sick and injured. Would you kindly come and tend to them?"

The colonel left without waiting for an answer. From behind the door, Dad heard Rotten Tomato jump up from his cot and scramble in his room to put on his uniform. Dr. Rotten Tomato ran to the waiting soldiers.

Later that evening, Colonel Hai summoned Dr. Rotten Tomato to the nightly staff meeting. The regimental doctors and medics normally stayed in the rear at headquarters, but Colonel Hai made an exception for Rotten Tomato. He instructed the doctor to accompany Dad on every field medical evacuation. Rotten Tomato no longer stayed in the aid station. The afternoon siestas were replaced with trips out to the frontline to deliver medical care. For the remainder of the time that Dad and Rotten Tomato were together, he made it a point to have the doctor wade through as many muddy rice fields as possible. Dad asked the helicopter pilot to hover over the muddiest spot or the roughest terrain and made the doctor jump out with him to the waiting soldiers.

TRIPS HOME DID NOT take Dad entirely away from the war. They did mean, however, that he could visit the prettiest girl in town. When he came to Mom's house to ask her parents for permission to marry her, they did not give him an answer. Eight nervous young men had come before him that year to ask for her hand in marriage. Mom did not have personal knowledge of her suitors. She did not have a boyfriend, in keeping with the custom and the wishes of her parents. The other suitors, like Dad, knew her from school, where her beauty captured the hearts of many eager young admirers. Mom had known Dad since elementary school, but she was not impressed by him or his high jinks. Nonetheless, he kept pursuing her. He waited for her outside of class to walk her home every day, although she ignored him. When Dad joined the army, he asked her to write to him.

Mom's parents were unsure how to respond to the suitors. They also did not want to lose their youngest child. Mom had an older brother and sister, both married adults when she was born. Consequently, Mom's parents doted on her and spoiled her like an only child. They curled her hair in ringlets to show off her cherub face and dressed her in dainty dresses when she was a little girl. Unlike most parents of that generation, where arranged marriages were common, they allowed her to decide on her spouse. Although they privately hoped that she would choose a nice young village teacher, she instead chose Dad.

On a clear April day in 1971, Dad, dressed in a dark suit and tie with a white pressed handkerchief tucked in his breast pocket, walked with his parents in a procession toward Mom's village home. His little brothers and sisters carried gifts of flowers and dried candied fruits wrapped

My parents celebrate their engagement in 1971. (Courtesy of Tran B. Quan)

in red cloth while his cousins carried a whole roasted pig. The traditional wedding ceremony began when Dad's clan arrived at Mom's house.

Her parents welcomed the guests inside. After the families exchanged gifts and nervous smiles, the room fell silent when Mom walked out escorted by her mother. She wore a traditional red silk *ao dai* that snugly hugged her slender frame. The floor-length garment swept along the floor as she walked out with hair pulled back in a chignon bun revealing the smooth delicate ivory skin on her face and neck. Dad greeted her with a shy smile and a bouquet of flowers. They both walked up to the home prayer altar to honor the family ancestors. With heads bowed, they said a silent prayer for a new life together, with Dad at twenty-three and Mom just twenty-one.

In the traditional tea ceremony, Mom's sister handed her a pot of chrysanthemum tea which she poured into a cup and offered to her in-laws as a sign of respect. Mom and Dad kneeled and bowed to their parents and elder relatives.

Due to the abundance of aunts, uncles, and cousins of multiple generations, mostly from Dad's side, the couple were obliged to kneel and bow for several hours. Dad bowed, nodded, and wiped the perspiration from his forehead. He promised to be on his best behavior, thinking all the while that his sweat and achy knees must make up for the pranks and trouble he had caused his relatives over the years.

After the tea ceremony, Dad changed into a fresh new shirt and Mom changed into a white wedding gown in style with the time. The wedding party moved to Dad's house for the reception, which stretched into the night and carried over to the next two days. Grandfather Luong footed the bill and spared no expense for his eldest son. He hired a crew of chefs that began cooking three days before the wedding. Over five hundred guests attended the lavish banquets, where they feasted on rich dishes like Peking duck, roast pork, and an array of seafood. To bless the couple's future together, symbolic food—such as sticky rice for happiness, fried spring roll for resiliency through the rough times, and boiled chicken for prosperity—was served.

The wedding party moved outside to a courtyard, festooned with glowing lanterns when nightfall came. Someone lit a burst of firecrackers, which rang in the jubilation. The crowd cheered at the eruption, but the popping noise that once thrilled Dad as a kid now jarred him. It brought him back to thoughts of battle which he wanted, at least temporarily, to escape.

The newlyweds honeymooned in the Central Highlands city of Da Lat, also known as the "City of Eternal Spring" for its year-round mild and cool weather. They hiked together through the green hills with towering pine trees, and they strolled through parks with natural lakes and waterfalls.

Sporting sunglasses and gold wedding bands, my parents honeymoon in Dalat, Vietnam. (Courtesy of Tran B. Quan)

They watched the mist roll over the valley from the balcony of their French colonial hotel room. Dad felt grateful that war had not yet ravaged the city. *What a shame,* he thought, *that the years of fighting destroyed the beauties of Vietnam and reduced them to burning villages and crumbled cities.* Yet, life continued with weddings and celebrations. From the hotel balcony, Dad wanted to stay in that moment—far away from war.

CHAPTER 8

Death

ON A BAD DAY for the 16th Regiment, Dad saw nearly forty dead bodies lying on tables made from the wood of discarded artillery crates, twelve inches tall and three feet wide. The sight of bloated corpses rotting from the heat did not bother Dad as much as the smell. On his first day inside the sheet-metal building with no air conditioning, the rank stench smothered him like a bag of rotten meat and garbage. He could taste the pungent odor in his mouth and throat. He wanted to vomit but maintained a cool, stoic face. The foul scent of death lingered with him long after the war.

Dad's assignment with the 16th Regiment bounced him back and forth from the battlefield to the mortuary. He transferred the wounded to the aid station and the dead to the morgue. His was the responsibility to identify and track the regiment's casualties. Identification of bodies became a challenge when fatal injuries mutilated the soldiers beyond recognition with dog tags blown or ripped off their bodies.

Vietnam at that time did not have resources like dental records to identify the dead. The job turned even more difficult when the deceased was a friend.

Villagers found one of Dad's closest high school buddies among a group of dead soldiers floating along a riverbank in summer 1972. This friend, Loc, had followed one grade behind him in school. They ran in the same circle of troublemakers.

Loc escaped death twice from Viet Cong ambushes, but he could not escape the third and final attack. The Viet Cong killed Loc along with twelve other soldiers, stripped their bodies of clothing except for their underwear, tied them to wooden crosses, and released them into the river. The dead bodies floated along the current for a week before villagers spotted the corpses. The bodies swelled to twice their original size and distorted the soldiers' physical features beyond recognition, with faces inflated to the size of watermelons and ballooned abdomens.

Dad searched for his friend among the dead but at first could not identify him. He and the platoon sergeant examined the pale dusky bodies, looking for any identifiable marks. Dad remembered that Loc had a long scar on the left shoulder blade from a mortar attack the year before. They turned each corpse over multiple times but could not see the scar. With each body that he turned, Dad felt a heaviness in his chest, as if doom had swallowed him. The lifeless and cold flesh did not scare him, but he dreaded and feared the discovery of losing another good friend. After a taxing search, they took a short break. The platoon sergeant left and returned with a bottle of whiskey.

The sergeant said, "Let's honor the dead brothers with a drink and a prayer for rest and peace." They gulped down a shot and prayed to find Loc's remains. Within minutes after the prayer, Dad spotted a body with a scar across the left shoulder blade. Sadness mixed with resignation settled over him as he looked at the grayish blue body. Each friend that he lost was like a page from his childhood ripped away by war. He notified Loc's family.

Loc's wife came to the morgue and with tears streaming down her cheeks confirmed her husband's body. She pointed to the only remaining article of clothing still on him—the boxer shorts she had sewed. The couple had only been married for less than a year.

Dad would see more war widows, some holding babies and small children, come to identify their husbands' bodies and collect the final small wage. Sometimes, he would dig inside his pocket, pull out his own money, and tuck it inside the palm of a child who lost a father. He knew the meager amount he offered only eased his own sadness but could not touch their loss.

Death became a constant threat that loomed over the lives of every South Vietnamese. Superstition and ghost stories invaded their minds and conversations. The tales helped them to reconcile and cope with the daily tragedies. In fact, before Dad came to the 16th Regiment it was known as the 13th Regiment. Its men insisted that the number thirteen was bad luck and requested another regiment number. Thus, the 13th changed to the 16th, which immediately boosted the morale and performance of its soldiers. The unit saw fewer deserters and a drop in disciplinary problems.

As a young lieutenant, Dad ignored the ghost tales. He entered in with the joke that the living can be scarier than the dead. However, things happen in life that make people reevaluate their beliefs from time to time.

Dad had his assertion tested during the first week of his arrival to the 16th Regiment barracks. The master sergeant handed him the key to his new quarters, the first room on the left in a series of rooms inside the American-style barrack. Before he left, the master sergeant gave Dad a worried look but didn't say anything.

Dad settled into the small room that had a twin-size bed and a table in a corner opposite the bed. He lit the kerosene lamp on the table to give the dark room light. He placed his bag of clothes inside a wooden box next to the door, then leaned his M2 carbine rifle against the wall at the head of his bed. He took his pistol and placed it under his pillow, a nighttime ritual he acquired before lying down to sleep.

After the third day, Dad ran into the master sergeant who asked, "How's the room?"

"Fine," Dad answered. But he noted the strange searching look in the master sergeant's eyes. Dad brushed it aside and went on his way.

Near midnight of the fifth day, Dad lay on his bed, not able to sleep. He stared out the small window into the dark starless night, then turned to the open barrack door. Dad felt a gust of cool wind blow across his body. He thought it odd for such a muggy night. Out of the corner of his eye he caught a vision of a dark shadowy figure draped in black shrouds hovering from the floor. It appeared manlike and Dad thought it was a Viet Cong at first, except it had no head. It lunged toward Dad and clutched his neck in a tight grip, not letting go. Dad struggled, kicking and flailing his legs while pushing against the specter. He tried to scream, but only a faint sound came out as he gasped for air. After what he guessed was two minutes of fighting but what felt like an eternity, the apparition released its hold and dissolved, leaving Dad drenched in sweat.

Even in the midst of disbelief, he remembered a Vietnamese superstition that he once mocked: ghosts feared dirty clothes. He took two pairs of dirty underwear and started swinging them back and forth in every corner of the room, trying to exterminate unwanted spirits. Soon after, he managed to fall asleep, mainly from exhaustion.

The next morning, Dad tried to make sense of the supernatural encounter. He hadn't drunk alcohol that day and was certain it wasn't a hallucination. Despite the grisly things he had witnessed in the service, he kept a sound constitution and doubted that he was having a mental breakdown.

The following day, he approached the army master sergeant and demanded, "Tell me about the room."

The sergeant chuckled. "It finally got you, huh?" He continued, "That room has a history. No one can stay in it more than a night. I'm surprised you made it almost a week."

The master sergeant revealed that the room had belonged to a second lieutenant who committed suicide with a rifle. He described the details to Dad. The young officer had killed himself over a broken romance. The deceased officer had rested the barrel under his chin while in the sitting position, and with his big toe pressed the trigger.

"I can give you a new room," the sergeant offered.

"I'd like to first offer a prayer to this lieutenant tonight," Dad answered, drawing on the traditional Buddhist practice of paying respect to the dead.

"I don't know if it would work, but you'd be the first to try," the sergeant said.

That night, Dad waited in the room with his pistol. He wasn't sure what to believe, but he was certain that whatever attacked him would be back. The master sergeant stopped by to sit with him. Dad placed a small dish with a few oranges and hard candy he bought that day on the table as a peace offering and said, "If you are the spirit of this lieutenant, I want you to know that you are pretty dumb, and you did a really stupid thing!" Dad continued to lecture while the master sergeant couldn't prevent a quiet chuckle. "No lover is worth killing yourself over. Was this girl the last woman on earth?"

Dad continued, "Listen to me. I outrank you and you need to obey my orders. Leave this room and go find your peace. I am not leaving this room. It has been assigned to me and that's final." Dad bowed his head as a sign of respect to the departed. He waited several minutes for a response, but not a breeze, a shadow, or a creak broke the calm silence in the room. After the master sergeant left, Dad tucked his pistol under his pillow and slumbered undisturbed that night.

The next morning, Dad went to a nearby Buddhist temple to offer a final prayer for the deceased. Before he entered through the opened weathered double doors, he heard the monotone chants of monks and the staccato sound of tapping on wooden drums. He couldn't catch the words of the meditative incantation, but the soothing sound anchored his mind. The scent of smoky sandalwood from the burning incense welcomed him inside. The fragrance was like the warm hug of a grandmother, something familiar and safe that he needed. He took off his shoes and placed them in a corner by the front entrance. The cool, smooth sensation of the stone floor under his calloused feet made him feel slightly vulnerable yet unguarded and free to release his burdens. Golden statues of Buddha and urns filled with lighted incense lined the walls. He cupped both hands together and bowed.

Dad lit a handful of incense, held it close to his chest, bent his head, and said a prayer. He prayed for the spirit of the departed to find peace; he prayed to live to see the end of the war; and he prayed for the protection of his soldiers. A feeling of peace entered him while the incense smoke twirled and rose into the air. Dad returned to his quarters and became its longest occupant. He kept that room for several years—until the war ended—without any other disturbance.

CHAPTER 9

The Soldier's War

"LIEUTENANT, BEFORE YOU punish a dog, you need to recognize its owner." The angry wife of Dad's commander wagged her sausage-shaped finger at his face and unleashed her wrath. Dad had thrown her son, a soldier in his platoon, into a tiger cage for several hours as punishment. The bamboo cages, used to contain tigers, were adapted by the North and South Vietnamese to punish prisoners. Dad knew his commander, Colonel X (whose true name will not be revealed), would not be happy. However, he did not expect this visit from the colonel's wife.

Dad responded, "Madame, I do not answer to you. I answer only to the army." With that, he walked away.

Dad had returned to the 9th Infantry Division after his honeymoon, and the duties of the army replaced those of married life. He fulfilled his military obligations and led his platoon without question. However, one sluggish and flippant soldier in his platoon—a soldier whose father commanded the regiment—did not respect the rules. Colonel X's son repeatedly showed up late for duty. After several verbal warnings that went ignored, Dad resorted to a common tactic used to punish disobedient soldiers of the time. He locked his commander's son in a tiger cage for several hours to bake under the sun.

Word of the encounter made its way back to Colonel X, who had already acquired a sordid reputation among his troops. While rumors circulated that Colonel X took bribes, his staff knew with certainty that when the colonel travelled by helicopter, he made his aide cover his seat with a cloth covered in embroidered dragons and tigers to symbolize his regal importance.

The tension between Dad and Colonel X reached the breaking point a day later when Colonel X rode out to confront Dad. The colonel came with two of his guards. Dad stood talking to his friend, a company commander in the regiment, when Colonel X pulled up in his jeep and hurled verbal attacks at Dad. He screamed, "How dare you throw my son in a tiger cage! You are a worthless traitor!"

Without saying a word, Dad looked the colonel in the eye, took off his metal helmet, and threw it to the ground. Colonel X fumed and ordered his guards to point their weapons at Dad.

Dad yelled to the guards, "Put down your guns!" They obeyed and backed off. The company commander who witnessed the showdown walked away, not saying a word. At that moment, the embarrassed colonel knew he had lost total respect and control of his men. He jumped in his jeep and sped away.

Dad stood firm in one place for some time, with both hands on his hips and head bent. He felt bad for himself and for the unit. Dad was not proud of his hot-headed reaction, but he did not regret it either.

Dad may have survived the showdown, but Colonel X found another way to exact his revenge. Dad was due for promotion to captain, but Colonel X made sure that he would not get promoted. He did so by giving Dad low marks on his officer evaluation report. The ARVN units, following protocol, kept the reports confidential from the rated soldier. Dad only discovered the result when the regiment's chief of staff, who couldn't believe the report himself, summoned Dad to his office and asked, "What happened, Le?"

The revenge turned out to be a mixed blessing. When the war ended, Dad remained a first lieutenant. A higher military rank would have guaranteed a stiffer punishment and longer imprisonment from the communist forces.

Despite the unfortunate encounter with one corrupt leader, Dad held great respect and affection for two of his commanding officers: General Di and Colonel Nguyen Van Hai, the 16th Infantry regimental commander, who preceded Colonel X. Intimidation never motivated Dad; instead, fairness and respect went a long way with him.

Colonel Hai's brawny frame towered over the average Vietnamese soldier. His generosity matched his high expectation for his men. He expected honesty and had a disdain for anyone faking knowledge. Colonel Hai had the patience to explain and teach for hours, but he hated anyone refusing to seek clarification for knowledge they lacked, whether from fear of inadequacy or laziness.

Colonel Hai liked Dad because the young lieutenant did not hesitate to admit what he did not know. The colonel had faith in Dad's abilities despite the shenanigans that he occasionally stirred. He recommended Dad to be the regiment's First Section Chief, which involved tracking the status of the unit's fighting force. Division headquarters offered Colonel Hai other more seasoned captains and majors to fill the position because they thought the twenty-four-year-old lieutenant was too green for the role. Colonel Hai refused and argued that Dad had the skills. The division relented. Dad worked hard to justify Colonel Hai's confidence in his abilities. He worked so hard that he did not eat properly, and the clothes that once fit snugly hung loosely on his shrinking frame after the first few months in his new assignment.

DAD HAD A BAD habit of borrowing money for cigarettes when his money ran out before payday. Of everyone from among whom he could have borrowed money in the regiment, he sought out Colonel Hai. The colonel could sense a request when Dad approached, scratching his head with a sheepish smile. This usually prompted Colonel Hai to ask, "You need money for cigarettes?"

With amusement, Colonel Hai said to his tank commander in front of Dad, "I can't believe this guy! He's the only one in the entire regiment who borrows money from me."

Regardless, Colonel Hai always reached into his wallet and handed Dad a little cash with a reminder, "Don't forget to pay me back when you get paid!"

Besides his generosity, Colonel Hai was also a spiritual man. He had a ritual upon arrival at each new place he and his troops occupied. As soon as they reached a new location, Colonel Hai gathered his soldiers around him. He announced, "I don't care if you are Catholics, Buddhists, or whatever religion you practice. We're all going to pray together."

He had his soldiers prepare the traditional Vietnamese prayer offering, which consisted of fruits they'd find in the market, like oranges and persimmons, and sometimes a few duck eggs, served on a small plate along with burning incense. Colonel Hai said a prayer to ask for the protection of his men. Traditionally, to seal the prayer, a Buddhist bell was clanged afterward. Since they didn't have a bell, Dad took two big empty artillery shells and banged them together.

Dad once asked Colonel Hai the purpose of those prayers. Colonel Hai answered, "I believe that each area is protected by spirits, and as guests we should make peace and pay our respects to the spirits."

When Dad received his promotion from second lieutenant to first lieutenant, Colonel Hai gathered the unit around the flagpole. He poured champagne from his personal collection onto Dad's new first lieutenant bars, polished them, then pinned them on Dad.

"I look forward to your next promotion," Colonel Hai congratulated Dad.

After the ceremony he gave Dad two bottles of cognac to celebrate. Dad planned to share his gift with the men in his regiment later that day.

Dad stood outside in the regimental headquarters dirt yard joking with his good friend, Second Lieutenant Quoi, a ranger in the regiment.

"Brother, I'm going to look for some snacks for your promotion meal after I return from doing security with my platoon," Quoi told Dad.

"You get the food, and I will supply the drinks," Dad offered.

Quoi gave Dad a quick wave and headed out of the regimental compound with his troops walking toward a nearby canal. Only two hundred yards away from where Dad stood, Quoi's platoon came under enemy fire from across the canal. Dad heard one loud blast. The machine gun bullet flew straight to Quoi's chest and shattered it. The soldiers ran, carrying his bleeding body, back inside the compound.

Dad rushed toward Quoi's motionless body. He tore open the blood-soaked shirt to apply pressure on the mutilated chest to no avail. Quoi, just twenty-three years old, died in Dad's arms.

That night, Dad sat alone with his drink. Colonel Hai stopped by Dad's quarters to console him. The colonel mused, "Such is the unpredictable life of a soldier. We live, die, and celebrate like brothers, never knowing when we will enjoy another drink together."

One early morning in 1973, as Dad made his way to the latrines, he spotted Colonel Hai standing alone at the regimental flagpole. Before the colonel raised the Republic of Vietnam flag to welcome a new day, Dad saw him embrace the yellow flag with its three horizontal crimson stripes— symbolizing the unifying blood that coursed through the northern, central, and southern regions of Vietnam. He wrapped both arms around the flag and held it tightly across his chest while visibly shaking and crying. Dad watched from a distance in silence; he understood. Colonel Hai was a man of great foresight who saw the beginning of the end for South Vietnam when the US withdrew its support in 1973. Colonel Hai knew that the South did not have the military power to battle on its own. Nonetheless, the country continued to fight alone for another two years while low on weapons, men, and supplies.

CHAPTER 10

The General's War

AFTER OUR BUFFET MEAL in Sarasota, almost everyone in the car fell into a food coma and dozed off except Cousin Hung, who had his strong brew of black coffee in the car cup holder. The ringing sound from General Di's cell phone woke us up.

"Hello, granddaughter!" General Di answered. His children and grandchildren called often during the trip to check on him. "I am having a wonderful time!" he reassured her.

Listening to General Di talk to his granddaughter, I felt confident that he treated his family, friends, and everyone else the same. However, I still wanted to know more about the man who was a father to five children and a father figure to ten thousand soldiers.

AS A BOY, DI waited every day for the pretty little girl with dark, twinkling eyes and long, glossy hair to
come by with her water pail. His parents' house was the
only home in the neighborhood that had indoor plumbing.
They allowed neighbors to come to the house to get water.
Every day she came to his house to fetch water for her family, and she would find him waiting. Sometimes she would
let him help her carry the buckets back to her house. That
was the beginning of their early, tender courtship.

People who laid eyes on Di as a young man remarked
that he was blessed with a handsome face that charmed
everyone even more when he smiled. He could steal the
heart of any girl, but his heart belonged to the little girl,
Doan Thi Be, with the twinkling eyes who lived down the
street. They married in 1955.

The couple started a family and had five children, four
sons and one daughter. Di continued his military duty,
which often took him away from home. Their busy and
happy life came to a halt when they experienced their first
family tragedy.

One of Di's soldiers rushed to his quarters to deliver
news from home. His family needed to speak with him. His
wife waited on the other end of the phone line. He tried
to follow her frantic voice as she explained the condition
of their second son who was taken that day to the hospital
with a high fever and cough. She sobbed while telling him
that the three-year-old became unconscious shortly after
arriving at the hospital. Then she delivered the blow that
knocked all his senses from him: his son was dead. He froze
with shock as his wife continued to weep.

Di came home to bury his son. The child's cause of death
was unknown, but the speculation was of an infection that
overwhelmed his body and airway.

At the funeral, people told Di that, among his five children, his second son had resembled him most. They shared

the same facial expressions, smile, posture, walk, and temperament.

The young family turned to prayer for healing. Di's faith in God and the comfort of prayer became the two constants in his life. Di would encounter the unexpected loss of another son thirty years later when his fourth child passed away from heart disease while just in his forties.

In the years between the loss of both sons, Di endured more personal grief. He drew strength from his Roman Catholic faith, his love for family, and the devotion of his military brothers to help him get through the pain.

Duty took Di away from his family for long stretches of time, but he found ways to remain a fixture in his children's lives. Every evening, he called home. The children lined up by the phone taking turns speaking to their father. He asked about their day and school. The children became accustomed to the daily calls but, as kids, did not see the significance of the ritual that their father tried to establish. Sometimes they fought to go first so that they could be free to go play with their friends. Yet the daily phone calls and his gentle voice reminded them that he cared.

When they heard the sounds of a helicopter landing on the sprawling yard outside the government-owned white stucco villa, the children knew that their father was home and lined up to greet him. They stood in formation with the oldest and tallest child up front, just like the children in *The Sound of Music.* Unlike the stern Captain von Trapp, however, Di met his children with a warm smile and a light embrace.

On some trips home, he carried a small bag—not filled with toys, to the disappointment of his children. Instead, he pulled from the bag a few yams and leafy greens, the same food that his soldiers ate. While the family had cooks to prepare their meals, he wanted to remind his children of their blessings versus the hardships that his soldiers endured.

During their simple meal of plain rice and boiled greens, Di explained to his children the Vietnamese saying: "One minute a person can be raised to sit on elephants and the next be lowered to the level of dogs." The old Vietnamese proverb conveyed the message of life's unpredictability. More important, he wanted to teach his children about the dangers of hubris, a lesson his father imparted to him years before. He told them, "Be grateful and humble despite life's fickle fortune."

BACK IN 1970 ON a spring morning, General Di took off from division headquarters in the command-and-control helicopter as he did most mornings after he took charge of the 9th Infantry Division. He routinely flew out with his helicopter pilot at six a.m. to survey battlegrounds. General Di used the information he gathered to plan airstrikes and arrange troop support. Flying at a low altitude, he often became a target for hostile antiaircraft weapons. His helicopter weathered multiple near misses. Up in the air, he thought about the frontline soldiers below, in more perilous conditions, forging through the waist-high water of rice paddies and booby-trapped jungles.

That morning, General Di planned for a stop at the 16th Regiment command post. From inside the bunker-turned-meeting room, Dad and the regimental officers could hear the general's helicopter land. Colonel Hai grabbed his hat from a table lined with other headgear sitting outside the bunker. In his rush, the colonel grabbed the wrong hat and ran outside to meet General Di. Colonel Hai didn't realize he wore a hat that belonged to a lower rank. He saluted General Di, who gave him an amused look and quipped, "Colonel Hai, when did you get promoted?" Dad couldn't restrain a chuckle.

After Colonel Hai briefed General Di on the regiment's status, the former ordered his soldiers to prepare a special lunch for their division commander. The general declined and opened a small sack tucked inside his olive-green nylon army bag. He pulled out two small boiled yams.

"This is all I need," Dad heard General Di say as he walked past. Having flown on frequent evacuation missions while dodging enemy fire from below, Dad knew that a full meal was not practical for some of the acrobatic flights. But more important, the humble image of General Di eating two simple yams comforted Dad when he and his soldiers went hungry on some missions.

A month later, General Di met up with Dad's regiment at a different command post in the rural countryside. This time, he traveled by jeep with just a driver and his constant companion: a portable communication radio. That day, General Di planned a visit to the 16th Regiment to ready the troops for a mission into Cambodia. The Viet Cong had long been in Cambodia, where they took advantage of sanctuaries along the Vietnam-Cambodia border in which they would hide, resupply, and return to Vietnam to continue their ambushes.

After reviewing the objective with the soldiers and officers, General Di solicited questions. Dad's friend, First Lieutenant Thap, nudged him, "Ask a question for me." Thap was fascinated with politics, always reading newspapers and magazines on the latest political intrigues.

"Ask him yourself," Dad countered, but he knew his friend's timidity as none of the other junior officers raised their hands.

"Next round of beer is on me," Thap promised.

General Di scanned the crowd gathered on the open field and saw one hand raised. He recognized the young lieutenant who mustered the gumption to ask for the use of his helicopter.

"Sir, what is your thought about the political infighting in the government and the military?" Dad repeated his friend's question and hoped he got it right. Everyone within ear's reach looked stunned. Dad regretted asking the question as soon as it flew out of his mouth.

"I serve the office of the presidency. I do not serve the person. I do not affiliate with any political party. I am country first," General Di answered in an even voice.

Before Dad and the soldiers of the 16th Regiment could digest the general's answer, they heard a faint, piercing sound like the screech of a shorebird growing rapidly closer—approaching from above—and they knew its origin. The soldiers ran for cover into bunkers and dove to the ground, covering their heads. Within three seconds the incoming mortar exploded twenty feet from where the battalion had stood. After the first mortar exploded, two more followed. While the troops raced for cover, Dad watched General Di walk at a smooth and steady pace toward the bunker.

When the artillery bombardment ended, the regiment assessed their field command post. The mortar bombs left smoldering gashes in the soil. Dad picked up a small shell fragment and examined the jagged sharp edges, still hot from the explosion. He did not have to imagine the intended consequences of the high explosives. Dad had seen his share of casualties with shrapnel lodged in eyes, face, and bodies. But on that day, luck spared them.

Dad heard boot stomps from behind and turned around to find his regimental commander and General Di.

"Is everyone safe, Young Brother?" General Di asked.

"Yes, sir."

"Do not hesitate to ask me for help. Even though I do not think that is a problem for you." General Di smiled and gave Dad a pat on the shoulder.

Before General Di departed for headquarters, Colonel Hai approached Dad and ordered, "Gather a dozen soldiers and escort General Di back, even if he refuses. If anything happens to him, Division will chew my flesh!"

Dad rounded up his platoon and piled them into two green army trucks, with one truck leading and another truck behind General Di's jeep.

A few miles from the destination, General Di waved from his jeep and signaled to the convoy, "Thank you, brothers! Safe return to your regiment." The trucks sat still for a minute, watching General Di's jeep drive out of their line of sight.

"Lieutenant, I've heard many good things about this general," the driver said to Dad. "They say he is tough but fair. And he cares about us."

Dad nodded and said, "I would follow him into any battle."

STARTING WITH A RIDE on a beat-up truck that broke down several times along the mountain road to the Cambodian border, followed by a stretch on a rented Lambretta motor scooter, A. J. Langguth made his way to Nui Sam, a town within a few miles of the Vietnam-Cambodia border, to catch up with General Di's troops. Langguth, a *New York Times* correspondent during the war, embedded himself with the ARVN 9th Infantry Division in summer 1970, during the division's operations into Cambodia, to write an article called "The Vietnamization of General Di."*

Langguth finally reached the 9th Division's command post with its clusters of tents pitched on a dirt trail. He found a group of Vietnamese and American officers dispersing from the command tent after a briefing. Before

* Vietnamization, a US strategy for the reduction of American involvement in the war by shifting the military burden to the South Vietnamese, resulted from American public pressure against an unpopular war. It paved the way for the eventual US withdrawal from South Vietnam.

meeting General Di, Langguth met with Colonel James Cavender, an American advisor.

Colonel Cavender asked Langguth, "Why, of the ten ARVN divisions, did you choose the 9th?"

"It was because of what I heard about its division commander, Tran Ba Di. He was said to be skilled and honest; best of all, he made no effort to court the press," Langguth answered.

"That's right," Colonel Cavender agreed. "He's such a solid guy; such a patriot. I was here for a full year, and he never asked for a bottle of booze or as much as a Pepsi."

Later in the day, Langguth found General Di standing alone at the side of a tent. He thought the general in his uniform looked taller than the average Vietnamese. Langguth introduced himself and asked the general how he pronounced his name: "Zee in the Northern manner or Yee [the Southern pronunciation]?"

"I say Yee. But either is correct." General Di followed his explanation with a hearty laugh. They talked about the mission and the weapon caches that his soldiers had recently captured.

General Di later told Langguth that he could try to catch the 16th Regiment in the Cambodian town of Tuk Meas to watch the operation.

Langguth met with ARVN officers in Tuk Meas who described the operation and their efforts to flush out the Viet Cong from the caves in which they were hiding with gas and grenades while seizing tons of ammunitions and antiaircraft guns. Then he wandered inside a medical tent and met Dr. Pham Van Chat, whom he described as "a melancholy young ARVN doctor with a beginner's mustache." Dr. Chat reported that they had lost thirty soldiers because they did not have enough helicopters to medevac the casualties out. Some had to wait more than twenty-four hours.

"When I told that to General Di, he turned away," Dr. Chat said. "He could not say anything. He was so sad he turned his face away."

Several days later, the 16th Regiment evacuated out of Cambodia. Langguth departed with them and headed back to division headquarters in Sa Dec, Vietnam. Langguth met with American advisors to discuss the strategy of Vietnamization.

Colonel Frank D. Connant revealed to Langguth, "I'm one of the great unwashed who thinks we're fighting here so we won't be fighting in San Francisco." Colonel Connant observed that, even though the 9th Infantry Division had its problems, it could stand on its own without US support.

By the end of July 1970, Langguth reported that the 9th Infantry Division, with assistance from the Vietnamese marines, rangers, and armored units, killed over 2,000 enemies and suffered fewer than 200 casualties. They captured 10,000 rifles and tons of ammunition.

Langguth wrote, "General Di's reputation rests on more than his kill ratio. Reporters who watched him move tanks and men through the Parrot's Beak last May considered his precision remarkable for the ARVN or any other army."

The anti-war movement in the US had gained momentum and accelerated the process for Vietnamization. However, the speed and rate of American troop withdrawal was a divisive issue among political and military leaders. General Di recognized the dilemma. He saw the South Vietnamese Army's resources stretched thin and feared that it would eventually reach a critical point when the Americans left. General Di worried that the US had trained the ARVN forces to fight like a United States army but without the resources once it left.

CHAPTER 11

The Advisors

NEARING FORT MYER, DAD kept watch for the exit that would take us off our road trip route and into the neighborhood where his friend, Cuc, lived.

"Did you know Major Cuc from division headquarters, General?" Dad asked.

"I am sorry, Brother, I did not," General Di answered. There were hundreds of officers at headquarters who had a special memory of General Di, as Dad did, but the general could not remember them all.

"He had a stroke last year, poor man," Dad said. "I've been wanting to visit him."

We arrived at a modest ranch-style house with two mango trees in the front yard. Expecting our visit, Major Cuc's wife waited for us by the door. She welcomed us inside. While Dad and General Di went straight to Major Cuc's bedroom, the rest of us sat waiting in the living room where statues of the Buddha sat on the mantel, with a few Christmas decorations scattered about to keep the house festive.

Dad approached Major Cuc's bed, where he lay para-
lyzed and unable to speak. His friend tried to utter a few
words but was unintelligible. Dad reached for Major Cuc's
hand and clasped it with both of his, holding on longer
than he normally would.

"Brother Cuc, do you remember our division commander?" Dad asked.

Major Cuc's eyes lit with surprise, and he acknowledged
General Di with a firm nod. General Di bent down and
gently patted Major Cuc's hand. Dad tried his best to stay
upbeat and joke with his friend as in old times, but he felt
the need for a beer and a cigarette to numb his sorrow. Dad
excused himself and went outside. General Di found him a
few minutes later.

"Younger Brother, true friendship is a precious thing,"
General Di stated. "It endures time, health, and background."
Dad felt grateful for those words, especially coming from a
man who gave and accepted friendship generously. The general nurtured bonds among his Vietnamese and American
brothers in arms of all ranks. His American allies never
forgot General Di's courage and warmth. Those friendships outlasted war, cultural differences, and separation.

IN 1963, VIETNAM'S MEKONG Delta, with
its mysterious maze of rivers, rice paddies, and villages,
lured the unsuspecting with its exotic beauty. One minute,
it disarmed the war-wearied eyes with the simple image of
a farmer plowing the muddy rice paddies with his water
buffalo, or of a village girl rowing a small wooden canoe
filled with green bananas along the canal. However, in the
deceptive calmness, the Viet Cong laid hidden in tunnels
and thickets, waiting to attack.

Captain John W. Nicholson arrived in the Mekong Delta
in 1963 to serve the first of three tours in Vietnam as an

American advisor to support a component of the ARVN known as the Civil Guard and Self Defense Corps (CG/SDC)* in Phong Dinh Province. The Mekong Delta was far from the Iowa farm that Nicholson grew up on and the familiar grounds of West Point that he knew as a cadet and faculty member. The Army sent him on assignments all over the world, but Vietnam's terrain and climate proved uniquely challenging. The unceasing rain of the monsoon season and the sweltering heat felt suffocating to the foreign troops.

The affable young captain quickly acclimated, though. He went on regular patrols with the Vietnamese soldiers, carrying two cartons of cigarettes. The two cartons would be gone by the next day as the Vietnamese soldiers called out, *"Hut toc, Dai Uy!* (A smoke, Captain!)" They liked American cigarettes, and they liked "Dai Uy Nick (Captain Nick)"—a title he fondly retained.

After the Geneva Accords were signed, President Dwight D. Eisenhower assured the new South Vietnamese government of US support, which included much-needed supplies, equipment, and the arrival of American advisors in 1955. The American advisors assisted Vietnamese forces with the acquisition of airplanes, weapons, ammunition, radios, and food. They coordinated what, where, and how much support was needed. They went on combat operations with the South Vietnamese forces and helped with the planning of the operations.

Dai Uy Nick's orders assigned him to the troops under the command of the then thirty-two-year-old Di, who held the rank of major and carried out the dual role of military officer and civil administrator as the province chief in Phong Dinh. Di shouldered the responsibility of providing

* The Civil Guard and Self Defense Corps were volunteer village militias recruited by the South Vietnamese military and organized into squads and platoons to provide security in villages and hamlets. They were considered to be an augmented component of the regular army.

government and military support to the citizens of the towns and villages of the region.

While most American service members had a difficult time communicating with their Vietnamese counterparts, Di's command of the English language and his pleasant nature made working partnerships and friendships easy. Dai Uy Nick and Di, naturally, became quick friends.

Then, in 1963, a lightning-fast ambush sealed their bond of brotherhood. During a land patrol on the Mekong Delta, shots from all directions came at them. A bullet took the life of Dai Uy Nick's assistant, and Di took a hit in the leg before he and his troops could return fire. Despite the pain and blood soaking his pant leg, Di continued to direct battle as bullets zipped past him. He yelled for his men to advance until the enemy retreated.

Once they subdued the enemy, Dai Uy Nick cut Di's trouser leg off. He applied a tourniquet and pressure bandage to the wound. Dai Uy Nick called for a medevac helicopter and told Di that they would transport him to an American hospital with surgeons.

Di responded, "No, Dai Uy. I must use the same doctors as my soldiers."

The soldiers carried Di to a bunker converted to an aid station. Sandbags lined the low-ceiling roof and the surrounding walls, a barrier to flying bullets. Wounded soldiers, clinging to life from the day's attack, lay on cots spread along the narrow room.

The makeshift aid station was equipped with little other than a few metal chests stocked with dressing bandages; it lacked any anesthetics. The wounded men's screams rang out often. The medics placed Di on a cot and tied both his wrists to the cot. After a quick examination of the hole in his leg, the Vietnamese doctors brought out a "cleaning rod," the same type used to clean the barrel of a rifle. They gave Di the end of a broomstick to bite on. With a swift stab, the doctor stuck the cleaning rod through the hole in Di's leg. Then they took a cloth bandage soaked with alcohol and ran it through the bullet hole. A strip of bandage came out of both sides of his leg. The doctor pulled the bandage back and forth through the hole, cleaning the wound. With his eyes shut tight, Di bit into the broomstick until it left deep teeth marks. Sweat poured from his head, yet not a profane word escaped from his mouth.

"You are lucky, Major, the bullet did not shatter a bone or tear a major blood vessel," the doctor told Di. They bandaged him up and moved on to the next wounded man.

Dai Uy Nick assured Di, "If your condition gets worse, I'll get the American doctors to come see you."

Di responded, "I am grateful, but do not do this unless I get very sick. I want the same treatment as my soldiers." Dai Uy Nick understood and found in this response another reason to admire his friend. Di rested alongside his troops, just as he wanted.

While Di could be firm and serious, Dai Uy Nick was aware of his witty sense of humor. Once Di's wound healed, he accompanied Dai Uy Nick on a mission to the countryside near an old French plantation. The miles of walking in the heat of summer exhausted them. Their growling stomachs reminded them they hadn't eaten since early morning. With dusk approaching, they made camp at the plantation before reaching their destination in the city of Can Tho.

The soldiers got out a frying pan and cooking oil. Dai Uy Nick could smell the aroma of the fried meat the soldiers were cooking. The Vietnamese soldiers liked sharing their food with Dai Uy Nick while he shared his cigarettes with them. When the frying was done, they gave him a helping of rice with bits of cooked meat. He took a bite and asked, "What kind of meat is this?"

"Bird meat," the soldiers answered. They offered him a second helping, and the strapping young captain with a hearty appetite eagerly accepted. Dai Uy Nick exclaimed, "Boy, these are really good! What kind of birds are these?"

Di gave his American ally a mischievous look and said, "Dai Uy, those are rat birds! But do not worry. We did a background check on every rat to make sure it was not a sewer rat. They are rice field rats!"

Several months later, in December 1963, Dai Uy Nick found himself in another ambush that would reunite him and Di forty-five years and ten months later. In a coordinated search-and-destroy operation in the northwestern remote rural region of Phong Dinh, Di's two hundred forty troops and their American advisor engaged the Viet Cong in the Song Hau Farm area. Di controlled the operation from a field command post several kilometers away.

Even though it was December, the temperature rose near ninety degrees Fahrenheit. The gunfire made the battlefield feel like a meat-grinding inferno. The ARVN soldiers took out two Viet Cong battalions and destroyed a hand grenade manufacturing site. Near late afternoon, the lead element of Di's troops reached a major canal, but this time the enemy overwhelmed them.

They took fire from all sides. Captain Phat, the Civil Guard commander, radioed the command post and reported the attack to Di, who immediately dispatched a gunboat to assist. When the gunboat arrived, the ambush intensified as the Viet Cong attacked from three sides with automatic weapons and mortar fire. Explosions, smoke, and rapid popping from guns cornered them. Mortar rounds landed on the gunboat while they were loading the casualties. One blast decapitated the machine gunner.

Frantic, the gunboat captain reversed and pulled away before all the wounded could be loaded. Chaos followed for the South Vietnamese as the enemy kept up their fire. Captain Phat's troops withdrew along the canal in the direction of the retreating boat.

Dai Uy Nick could not leave the wounded troops on the canal bank. He ordered his interpreter, Khiem, to urge Captain Phat to retrieve the wounded.

Nighttime set in as Captain Phat's remaining troops returned for their comrades. The moon and stars hid behind a blanket of clouds that left the Mekong Delta in pitch blackness. Once they established security, Dai Uy Nick and the remaining thirty-nine troops forged through the countryside and found the thirteen wounded soldiers. Dai Uy Nick and the troops carried the injured for five hours that night northward to safety. Four of the wounded died en route, but their bodies were carried nonetheless. The Viet Cong continued to fire at them from three directions. They returned fire to their flanks and rear. The support from the friendly mortar rounds kept them from being boxed in. By two the next morning, Dai Uy Nick and the troops reached the safety of the command post.

Shortly after, Di awarded Dai Uy Nick the Vietnam Cross of Gallantry with Gold Palm, the highest level of ARVN military decorations. Unbeknownst to Dai Uy Nick, the US military also initiated paperwork for him to receive the Silver Star, but he would not receive it until over forty-five years later. The paperwork got lost and had to be resubmitted. Dai Uy Nick's former "Paddy Rats" commander, Lieutenant General John Cushman, reached out to General Di in 2008 for a statement to support Dai Uy Nick's valor. In 1963, General Di sent Dai Uy Nick artillery support. In 2008, General Di sent his support with words from the stroke of his pen.

On October 28, 2009, General Di traveled from Florida to be with the crowd of family and friends who gathered at Fort Myer, Virginia, to watch General Cushman pin the Silver Star on Dai Uy Nick's chest. General Di brought with him a pair of Mickey Mouse socks as a gift for his friend to go along with the Silver Star.

General Di shares a meal with the American advisors during a break from the fighting in 1963. General Di with his back to the camera; Captain "Mac" McFarland to his right. (Courtesy of Harry McFarland)

HARRY "MAC" MCFARLAND JOINED the US Army at eighteen. He packed a Canon camera, ready to capture the new places and people he hoped to discover. The Army took him far away from the woods of Pennsylvania where he had hunted and roamed as a boy. It brought him to Germany in the 1950s, where he met and served with Dai Uy Nick. The friends reunited in the Mekong Delta in 1963, advising the forces under Di. Similar to his friend Dai Uy Nick, Captain McFarland became known to the Vietnamese soldiers as "Dai Uy Mac."

During breaks from the fighting, Dai Uy Mac volunteered to teach English to a class of Vietnamese villagers. The motley group of students, ages ten to sixty, looked at the blond-haired, blue-eyed American officer with curiosity. Why did he care about teaching them English? The Viet Cong who came to their village told them not to trust the "evil" Americans, but they liked Dai Uy Mac. He was

nothing like the Viet Cong's description. Laughter ener-
gized his classroom as students and teacher tried to learn
one another's language and culture.

Dai Uy Mac was equally intrigued. When he wasn't
fighting or teaching, he wandered around with his 35mm
camera taking pictures of village life. His camera captured
images of straw and bamboo homes along a serene riverbank, the tears on the face of a war widow, and schoolchil-
dren running toward him at the end of class. His camera
and the pieces of candy he brought along won over the
children and villagers in a way that the Viet Cong propaganda and threats could not.

He went out on operations with Di to visit troops and
villagers in the Mekong Delta. During these trips, Dai
Uy Mac observed the poorest villagers embrace Di with
a warmth he recognized as one that only time and trust
could earn. He reported back to his American peers that
while Di wielded a tremendous amount of influence and
power in the province of Phong Dinh, "Di was not the type
of leader who screams or growls. People gave him what he
wanted because they respected him so highly." Dai Uy Mac
returned from the missions with Di inspired to bring light
to a dark time.

At the end of Dai Uy Mac's tour, his students gathered
around him on the last day of class and surprised him with
a watercolor drawing. For days the students planned in
secret how they could show him their appreciation. They
picked the best artist in the class to paint the picture. At
the bottom of the picture, they penned a message with the
English he taught them. Tears came to Dai Uy Mac's eyes
when saw the painting. It illustrated him working in a rice
paddy, planting seeds of "Love." The inscription at the bottom of the picture read, "...*with heart and soul. . . . To the best
of my knowledge, one sows knowledge and the other plants love.
God bless them!*"

After Vietnam, Dai Uy Mac went on to serve twenty years with the Army and retired as a lieutenant colonel. He carried the picture back to America where it hung in his Oregon den for fifty-plus years.

ON A DRIVE THROUGH the rural Cang Long District, in 1962, Arthur E. Brown Jr. asked his driver to stop at a Buddhist pagoda beside the road. Intrigued by the Vietnamese people and culture, Brown stepped out of the jeep and walked toward the shrine. He wanted to know more about the land he was sent to help as a part of the Military Advisory Assistance Group-Vietnam (MAAG-V).* His driver, Thong Hong Tran, a lanky ARVN soldier in his twenties with suntanned skin and high cheekbones, beckoned the American captain back to the vehicle. Neither could speak the other's language and communicated by hand signals and a few Vietnamese words. Dinh, the Vietnamese interpreter, rode along and provided the translation. The three became a close team and traveled throughout the Mekong Delta during Brown's first tour.

On the drive back to headquarters from Cang Long, Thong's mind drifted to his wife and kids after Brown shared pictures of his family in America. The three men accustomed themselves to the bumpy waves of the dirt road, along which they would not see a car for miles, making it serenely desolate. Then, from nowhere, a rooster unexpectedly flew straight into the front of their jeep. Thong couldn't dodge it and ran over the bird.

He continued driving, leaving the dead rooster in the rearview until Brown told him, "Stop! Stop!" Brown pulled out money from his wallet, gesturing that they must compensate the rooster's owner.

---

* Military Advisory Assistance Group designated US military advisors sent to other countries to assist in the training of armed forces and to facilitate military aid from the 1940s through the 1970s.

Thong did not feel the same. To him, it was a minor accident not worth the trouble. Nonetheless, they got out of the vehicle and found the rooster's owner at Brown's insistence. With a crowd of amused villagers around them, Brown's interpreter explained that the American officer wanted to pay for the dead rooster. Thong heard some of the villagers scoffing, "It's nothing to fuss about." But he knew from the approving looks on other villagers' faces that Brown's action left a respectful impression on them all.

It only took Thong a short time to form an opinion of the American officer. He saw Brown refusing to send in planes to bomb a church with known Viet Cong hiding inside. Instead, Brown gave orders to release a shower of bombs around the church perimeter that sent the Viet Cong scattering into the jungle—as Thong remembered, "like a flock of geese released from a cage." Thong watched Brown chase after the Viet Cong into the jungle. While bullets flew, Brown refused to take cover and shot back until the enemy was subdued. He seemed fearless to Thong.

Before he returned to America near the end of 1963, Brown had one more task to check off. He noticed that Thong pedaled to work every day on a rickety bicycle with scratched paint and rusty chains. Like most Vietnamese, Thong could not afford a car. To get a more advantageous price, Brown asked Dinh to look around for the best bike with the finest parts. The American captain knew that the vendors would overcharge him if he went himself.

Brown kept Thong's gift a secret, even from Dinh. Not knowing the bike's recipient, Dinh delegated the task back to Thong. With instructions only to spare no expense on the finest bike in the city, Thong returned with a sharp white chrome bike. He showed the bike to Dinh and thought the bike's owner would be one lucky person.

Brown admired the bike with Thong and Dinh and playfully told them that he planned to ship it home to America.

But he asked Thong to try it out first. Thong sat on the comfortable seat and his face reflected off the shiny new chrome handlebar. Then Brown pulled out his camera and took a picture of Thong on the bicycle to show his family in America.

When Thong attempted to hand the bicycle back, Brown said to him, "It's for you."

THONG WOULD NOT FORGET his American friend. Their paths crossed again some years later, in 1969, when Brown returned to Vietnam for his second tour as a lieutenant colonel. By then, Thong had made the decision to return to school and become an officer. He completed the ARVN's Officer Candidate School (OCS) and worked his way up the ranks. This time the two men's paths led them to Di, who had achieved the rank of brigadier general.

In April 1970, Lieutenant Colonel Brown crossed into Cambodia with General Di's division, conducting operations to seek and destroy Viet Cong weapons and supply caches. On June 30, 1970, all US advisors had to leave Cambodia by midnight. General Di helped supply helicopters to get all the advisors out. Years later, Brown summed up General Di's action by stating, "He treasured life."

For Thong, it was General Di's understanding for life that he remembered. Thong witnessed that quality in his first encounter with General Di in 1973, during a reprimand at the IV Corps Headquarters where he and a group of officers attended a two-month training course. Thong often raced home to his family on most weekends but arrived back late one Monday morning. The instructor called Thong, along with a handful of his classmates, to explain their tardiness to the IV Corps Deputy Commander, General Di. When it was Thong's turn to explain, he gave General Di a frightened look and said, "General, I miss my wife and kids. This is the first time in my ten-plus years with the army that I've screwed up."

"How many times did you say?" General Di asked.

"Just this once, sir, in over ten years," Thong answered.

"To screw up is to be human." General Di gave them an amused smile. He sympathized with his troops, understanding that the decades of war had become part of their daily existence and knowing that his soldiers had to find ways to cope. However, in the same breath he warned the group that if their actions continued, he would fail them from the course.

BROWN RETURNED TO AMERICA in July 1970 to continue his thirty-six-year career in the Army, which earned him the rank of a four-star general and elevated him to the position of Vice Chief of Staff of the US Army (1987–1989). Along with the medals he acquired from Vietnam, Brown took with him lasting memories of Thong, Dinh, General Di, and the ARVN commanders who refused to surrender. However, after 1975, he lost contact with them when they disappeared into the communist prisons.

In his retirement, General Brown took up cycling. Three days out of the week, he rode thirty to forty miles with a cycling group on a bicycle he named "Blue Max." In 2016, at age eighty-six, he led a sixty-two-mile bike ride for the Boys and Girls Club of Hilton Head Island. Sometimes on his bike rides, he thought about Thong and the Vietnamese friends in his past.

The end of 2016 going into 2017 became a time of reunion for General Brown and the South Vietnamese brothers he'd known. General Brown discovered that General Di lived an hour away from his daughter in Florida.

He wrote General Di a letter recalling exact names of their Vietnamese acquaintances and events over decades ago. The two spoke on the phone with plans for a visit.

A few months before reconnecting with General Di, General Brown received an unexpected phone call late one December night from another friend in his past: Thong, who had immigrated with his family to the US in 1996. Upon his arrival to America, Thong searched for General Brown with the help of his youngest son, Khai. As they spoke, Khai saw the tears well up in his father's eyes when General Brown asked, "Do you remember the bike?"

Thong remembered the treasured gift. The bike remained intact and in use to the day he left Vietnam. Before Thong immigrated to America, he handed the bike over to his brother-in-law and made him promise never to throw it out. Thong told him, "Keep the frame even if the rest of the bike falls apart."

There is a Vietnamese phrase, *tinh nghia*, whose literal translation is "bond" and "duty." When used together, these two words form an expression that symbolizes deep loyalty and kinship to another person. General Di's American advisors showed *tinh nghia* to him and the people of South Vietnam.

CHAPTER 12

The Fall

WHEN TWILIGHT FELL, THE setting sun and his fatigue made the road harder for Cousin Hung to navigate. He reached for his coffee cup and saw that it was empty. He spotted a rest stop along the Florida highway and pulled in. Next to the public restroom, he saw a coffee vending machine—two necessities for the weary traveler.

With paper cups of coffee in hand, Dad, General Di, and Cousin Hung stood by the vending machine sipping their beverages. I walked around the rest stop, staying near the lighted area. The brightest illumination came from the flagpole where the American flag, and underneath it a black POW/MIA flag, flew. I approached the coffee drinkers and pointed to the flagpole.

"Shouldn't the flags be lowered at sunset?" I asked.

"It can still fly at night as long as it is well lit," General Di answered.

Our attention stayed on Old Glory and the POW flag, steadily flapping in the evening breeze.

"Our South Vietnamese flag was not even given the dignity to be properly lowered. It was just ripped off on the last day," Dad said with a wistful look.

"And we became the living symbol of prisoners of war in our own land," General Di added.

NEAR THE END OF April 1975, the yellow apricot blossoms that came each spring to South Vietnam withered away from the intense heat of artillery fire. The intensity of the dry season built up like an anger that brewed until it spilled over in tears as the monsoon rain came in May. General Di sensed the breaking point nearing for South Vietnam as did other high-ranking government and military leaders that spring.

A week before the last day of April 1975, General Di prepared for work as he had most mornings since he became the commander of Quang Trung National Training Center, the largest preparatory center for ARVN soldiers. The new position took him away from the active military combat to head training for approximately 20,000 recruits in November 1974. General Di was not given reasons for his transfer from his position as Deputy Commander of the IV Corps to the new assignment. He had the experience and the results to lead an infantry division and a corps. General Di suspected that politics got involved. Yet, he never cared to participate in the power struggles. He simply continued to do what the military asked. He told himself that if the order were not unethical, "a good military officer will salute and do or go" as directed, even if he or she does not like it. He missed being involved in the combat units, but the change of assignment meant less time away from his family.

On most mornings he ate a simple breakfast of rice porridge and promptly left for work. But that dawn, he lingered longer by his family's side. Underneath his calm exterior, a storm of worries brewed. There were things he wanted to say to them, but instead he asked his wife, "Could you make me my favorite dish this morning?"

His wife, surprised by the rare request, sent the cook to market for ingredients to make *mam va rau*, a traditional Vietnamese hot pot dish made with shrimp, pork belly, fish, eggplant, and Vietnamese herbs. The invigorating scent of lemongrass merged with the warm aroma of garlic, onion, and seafood flowing from the kitchen made the unassuming morning festive. Yet only known to General Di, it was perhaps a farewell meal with the people he treasured most. No one suspected, not even his wife. He was good at keeping secrets.

From the dining room table, he could hear the busy kitchen sound of chatter from his wife and the cook along with the chopping, slicing, and bubbling from the pot. He watched his children seated at the table, healthy and hardy, jabbering away about an upcoming shopping trip. His heavy heart wished that simple moment would last longer than the short hour it took to prepare the meal. He asked his children about their plans that day, savoring each moment with them.

"Shoe shopping in Saigon. We need sturdy shoes to run from the communists in an attack," his teenage daughter, Que Huong, answered. He looked in silence at the bowls and chopsticks set on the table. Her words sent him deep into his own worries.

The approaching aroma of his favorite meal brought him back to the table when his wife carried out the large pot of seafood stew and placed it in front of him. A kitchen staff carried the accompanying side dish of rice noodles and baskets of banana flower, beansprouts, and lime. Di ladled a good portion of stew into each child's bowl before serving himself and his wife. He relished the sounds of their slurps and the crunch made from the beansprouts and ultimately joined them, but with a less hearty appetite. While his family ate, he made a mental note of the moment and locked it away, remembering it later during his most trying times.

Just before his family set out for shopping that afternoon, General Di's assistant arrived at the house. He told the family, "You must leave for the airfield now! It is an order from the general."

There was no time to pack. Scared and stunned, they obeyed and squeezed into an awaiting car that whisked them to the airport. They felt the urgency of the order echoed in the distressed voice of the general's assistant and did not question it. Once at the airport, they saw families of American and Vietnamese officials also trying to leave Vietnam. The day was one week before the official fall of South Vietnam. The mission to evacuate families of key military and government officials out of Vietnam was still hushed.

The defense attaché official at Tan Son Nhut Air Base handed an orange phone to General Di's wife and children. They heard his voice on the other end as each said their hasty goodbyes. He wanted to say more but worried that the lines might be monitored and would jeopardize their escape. His wife pleaded with him to leave with them.

He told her, "I must stay with my soldiers. Take care of the children. I will see you again." After the quick call, his family rushed into a plane that flew them to the US naval base in Subic Bay, Philippines. They stayed in Subic Bay for two days before they were transferred to a military base in Guam. The sudden whirlwind left them shocked but safe.

"SIR, THE COMMUNISTS HAVE advanced into Saigon," the liaison officer informed General Di on April 27, 1975.

"We need to set up attackers to defend the training center," General Di responded. In addition to training soldiers, the center also trained truck drivers, which gave them access to light trucks, heavy trucks, and eighteen-wheelers. He used the big trucks to set up anti-tank mines beneath the road and brought out the anti-tank weapons. When two communist tanks rolled toward the training center, they destroyed the tanks.

With three divisions still intact—the 7th, 9th, and 21st—General Di believed they could continue the fight. He called the military capital special command headquarters in Saigon, but no one answered. Without hesitating, he jumped into a jeep with his driver and went into the capital. General Di arrived at three p.m. on April 29 to an empty headquarters. He learned from radio communication that all general officers were ordered to report to the Joint General Staff (JGS) headquarters. He could not reach the JGS due to the chaos on the roads. A sea of humanity flooded the routes out of Saigon, fleeing for their lives. He could hear exploding rockets and gunfire in the distance and see smoke rising from the wreckage.

That night, he stopped at his uncle's house in Saigon and called back to the training center. No one answered. Everyone had fled. In the morning, General Di reported to a military post in Saigon. He told the commanding officer, the only officer still at the post, that he could not report to the JGS headquarters.

At 3:30 p.m., April 30, 1975, Duong Van Minh, who had been president for only three days after his predecessor Nguyen Van Thieu resigned and fled to Taiwan, announced on a radio broadcast, "I declare the Saigon government . . . completely dissolved at all levels." In Guam, General Di's wife and children huddled together with a group of Vietnamese refugees, known as the lucky one percent, who escaped Vietnam before the surrender, listening to the announcement by radio. They had no news of General Di. They did not know if he were captured or even still alive.

On April 30, 1975, the enemy came out from the darkness of night to seize the capital of South Vietnam by daylight. Their nighttime acts of sabotage ultimately led the communist troops to advance to Saigon at daybreak, the victors of a bitter two-decade war. When the North Vietnamese troops barreled into Saigon, they rammed their tanks against the gates of the capital's Independence Palace—South Vietnam's equivalent to the White House. Then they plastered their flags and a picture of Ho Chi Minh onto the palace wall.

Desperate South Vietnamese rushed the US Embassy gate to get onto packed helicopters perched atop the embassy's roof. The overflowing helicopters took them to safety on the waiting US military ships. Those in the government and military who remained at their posts tried to maintain order amidst the chaos as rockets and gunfire pounded Saigon. The day still came as a shock to many South Vietnamese patriots who could not accept defeat, despite the odds. Many ARVN leaders and soldiers took their own lives on the final day of the war. For them, death was a better option than surrender.

"BURN ALL PERSONNEL RECORDS and classified documents!" Dad shouted to a drove of soldiers hauling out all the metal barrels in the regiment on that night of April 30, 1975. He ran into the headquarters' main office and helped another crew of soldiers empty file cabinets and carry boxes of documents outside where they were dumped into the metal barrels.

They poured gasoline on the mountain of paper and threw in a lit match. A burst of flames shot into the air.

They continued to fuel the fire with boxes of military records. The night breeze lifted the burning ashes into the air like glowing fireflies in the dark. Documents that captured ranks, date of army entry, assignments served, disciplinary actions, and citations of bravery evaporated into smoke and ashes.

Earlier that day, Dad had attended the monthly division meeting in Vinh Long. Halfway through, the division chief of staff, Colonel Pham Van Ven, was summoned out of the meeting. He returned, face ashen, and announced "It is over; we have surrendered."

A stunned silence enveloped the room until Colonel Ven directed the men back to their units to await further orders. Dad walked out of the meeting feeling like he received the last blow of a grueling brawl. His knees felt weak, as though they wanted to buckle, as he walked toward the jeep. By the time he reached his regiment, everyone had learned of the surrender from the radio announcement made by the acting South Vietnamese president. Dad saw officers and soldiers crying like they were at a funeral. For them, the surrender was a death.

The regimental commander ordered the troops to lay down their weapon. But before surrendering their arms, the soldiers engaged in one last act of defiance against the enemy. They took out the bolts and firing pins of their rifles, making the guns useless. They threw the defective weapons into a giant pile and waited.

"They'll find a way to punish us all," Dad's friend First Lieutenant Muoi said. They stood together, watching the flames shoot from the metal barrels that night, waiting for morning and the communists to roll in.

Dad answered, "We'll make it harder for them."

"In that case, let's open up the food warehouse to our soldiers and their families. I don't want it to go to the communists," Muoi suggested. They sent word to the two hundred military families living near headquarters that they could get as much rice, flour, and cooking oil as they could carry. By three a.m. the families had cleaned out the warehouse.

At eight a.m., Dad saw a reduced battalion of one hundred twenty North Vietnamese soldiers advancing toward their last defense line, several hundred yards from the garrison gate. The communist forces intercepted the ARVN's 16th Regiment's radio frequency and delivered their demands before entering. They ordered the defeated soldiers and officers to line up in formation. The fear of a mass execution entered the thoughts of the men in the 16th Regiment.

"We could take them. We still have enough ammunition. There's two hundred of us here, and there's no more than a hundred of them out there," Dad said to Muoi.

Muoi answered, "Our regimental commander and the president of Vietnam declared an unconditional surrender. The enemy didn't send many soldiers to take us down because it's over."

Within minutes, the North Vietnamese stormed into the garrison screaming profanity. They ransacked the headquarters while the South Vietnamese troops stood awaiting their fate. The communists pulled out office drawers and personal lockers to loot for valuables. A few of them found washed clothes and stuffed them into their pockets.

Muoi whispered to Dad, "They look like mismatched pirates."

The victors wore homemade-type uniforms of black and green cloth. The officers had sandals with soles made from old truck tires strapped to their feet. The soldiers went barefooted.

A North Vietnamese officer, whose eyes flashed with hatred, approached Dad and pointed a flare gun to his head. Dad felt the pressure of cold metal against his temple. "You can still wear your sunglasses during your time of shame?" the officer questioned with a smirk.

Dad felt his heart throbbing in his throat but managed to respond, "They're not sunglasses. They're tinted vision glasses."

The man yanked Dad's glasses off and stuck them in his pocket, then screamed at the men of the 16th Regiment, "You are traitors to your country! You've been brainwashed and fooled by the West! Go home. You will receive instructions soon. We will kill you if you try to escape. We have citizen spies all over!"

GENERAL DI TRIED TO fight back acrid tears when he heard the call, by the president of South Vietnam, for every man to lay down his arms and wait for the communists to come. While the government, the military, and any semblance of order in South Vietnam unraveled, General Di refused to accept defeat. For the first time in his military career, he refused an order. He changed out of his military uniform into civilian clothes, placed his belongings in a sack, and ditched his military jeep. He had to find an unmarked vehicle to make his way to the divisions further south. He found a ride with a soldier's family fleeing Saigon. They joined a mass of people making an exodus out of the capital. He wanted to get on the highway to head back to the Mekong Delta, where he believed there were still three viable divisions with fearless corps commanders.

People jammed onto the roads in a feverish rush, using all forms of transportation: cars, trucks, buses, motorbikes, ox carts, bicycles, and by foot—carrying baskets and sacks and with children in tow. As they fled, exploding bombs filled Saigon's horizon with smoke, and communist tanks thundered into the city. The throng of people did not get far before a roadblock stopped them. The communists made everyone get out of their vehicles with keys left in the ignition and marched the group to an open field three hundred meters from the road. Men, women, and children huddled together. General Di waited with the trembling group while very much aware of the communists' history for massacres. He heard adults sobbing as they prayed and children whimpering. He placed his hand over his concealed pistol, waiting for the next move.

A communist soldier announced to the crowd, "You will pledge your allegiance and gratitude to the new government." General Di unclenched his hand and mumbled along. The soldier led them in a chant that they had to repeat over and over for an hour before he released them. They returned to find an empty road. The communists had confiscated the vehicles. The only personal item General Di had left was his concealed pistol.

General Di joined the crowd of stranded travelers and headed down the road. Men and women, young and old, trudged aimlessly along, some with babies on their backs or in their arms. The older children toted the younger ones. The escapees had grave looks of fear in their eyes.

They walked several miles until they came across an abandoned bus that still had its keys, likely deserted from the series of communist roadblocks. General Di asked, "Does anyone know how to drive the bus?" No one volunteered. He took the wheel and drove the bus, packed with people, south toward My Tho, where the 9th Infantry Division had a mobile command post. He drove for twenty kilometers until they hit another roadblock. Once again everyone got off the bus and followed the same drill from the previous roadblock. After more chanting, they were allowed back on the road, but without a bus.

General Di walked with the crowd of exhausted and dejected adults and children. Trucks racing south passed them without stopping. When one open cargo truck slowed down, General Di saw his chance and jumped onto the back. He reached My Tho that night alone, but he could not enter the command post. He did not see ARVN soldiers guarding the front but heard voices with northern accents cursing the people of South Vietnam. At that moment, he knew that the communists had full control of the 9th Infantry Division.

That night, he snuck to his parents' house nearby. They pulled him inside, relieved to see him still alive. The next morning, he asked his sister to drive him to the IV Corps Headquarters in Can Tho.

When General Di and his sister arrived, nothing stirred outside the massive compound except the Republic of Vietnam flag waving defiantly in the wind. The two brick buildings still had the scent and remnants of life, but without its people. Typewriters with fresh ink ribbons sat on desks next to stacked memos dated only a few days before. Offices appeared undisturbed, as if the owners would return the next day, except for empty file cabinets with missing records that had been whisked away.

When Di entered the headquarters, there was emptiness and silence. He walked down the halls but could not see another human form or hear a human voice. The only sound came from the thud of his boots. The silent eeriness made him feel even more alone. Then an aide to the corps commander appeared from an office and broke the silence. "General Nam and his deputy, General Hung, refused to surrender and took their own lives."

The IV Corps Commander Major General Nguyen Khoa Nam and his Deputy Commander Brigadier General Le Van Hung met with distraught citizens of Can Tho on the evening of April 30. The people pleaded for the ARVN forces not to fight to the death as they knew the soldiers would. The citizens feared that the communists would spare no one and shell the city into ashes until they achieved victory. Generals Nam and Hung did not want to inflict more civilian deaths and suffering, so they relented.

The two men, however, would not personally surrender to the communists. Shortly after meeting with the people of Can Tho, General Hung said farewell to his soldiers, wife, and children. He killed himself with a .45 pistol at 8:45 p.m. on April 30, 1975. His commander, General Nam, bid farewell to his staff and took his life at 11:30 that night.

Heartbroken, General Di returned to his parents' home. Several communist officers and soldiers waited for him in his parents' living room. With masked contempt, they told him, "Brother, the war is over. Report to our 9th Region Headquarters when you receive instruction."

As soon as the communists left, General Di hopped on a motor scooter with his younger brother and raced one hundred miles south from their hometown to the coastal city of Rach Gia that looks out into the Gulf of Thailand. They drove nonstop, pushing the scooter to maximum speed. They planned to take a boat from Rach Gia to Thailand. General Di knew that the city was still loosely guarded by the communists. In the first few weeks immediately after the surrender, chaos prevented the communists from exerting their full grip across the South. Movement from Vietnam to Thailand by boat was still possible. When they reached Rach Gia, General Di and his brother tried to blend in with the crowd waiting at the dock to board a fishing boat.

A former South Vietnamese police officer, still in uniform, also waited with the crowd. When the communist guards appeared for a random check, the police officer thought they were after him. He panicked, pulled out his revolver, and shot one of the guards. People in the crowd screamed and scattered. The second guard returned fire and shot the police officer. A group of communist soldiers rushed to the scene and rounded up everyone at the dock. They stopped all movement in Rach Gia. They interrogated everyone in the group and uncovered General Di's identity. His plan for escape ended that day. Three days later, he reported to a detention camp in Can Tho where his troops once held communist prisoners during the war. Entering the detention camp, he muttered to himself, "This is an irony of fate."

THE COMMUNISTS RELEASED THE lower-ranking South Vietnamese soldiers but forced Dad and the officers of his regiment to strip down to their white t-shirts and boxer shorts. Uniforms and boots were confiscated. They sent the officers home in their underwear to signal the beginning of the long humiliation ahead.

Dad climbed into the back of the tuk-tuk cab* crammed with passengers, heedless of his attire of underwear and sandals. The people around him did not seem to care either; their world had just turned upside down that day. Dad asked the driver to take him to Grandfather Luong's home in Vinh Long, first.

The streets of Vinh Long had a mournful air but lacked the hysteria of Saigon. Few people ventured out, and the ones that Dad saw looked the way he felt—lost. The tuk-tuk dropped him off at the steps of his parents' house. Grandfather Luong stood outside the front door, as if knowing that his son would be coming home. Dad did not have to say a word; the disheartened look on his face was enough. Grandfather patted him on the shoulder and shook his head while staring at the ground. The light touch of comfort was the most physical affection that Grandfather would show even though his heart overflowed with love for his eldest son. There was no big hero's homecoming, just a dejected soldier who had done his part. Regardless, Grandfather Luong had his son alive and home. He remembered the youthful confidence in Dad's voice when

---

* Tuk-tuk: a motorized vehicle, usually three wheeled, adapted from the traditional pulled or cycled rickshaw.

he entered the army seven years before, telling his parents, "Don't worry. I'll make it out safe."

Before he left the regimental headquarters that day, Dad told his friends, whose clothes were all confiscated, to stop by his father's house. He had spare clothes stored there to give them. He selected one outfit for himself and gave the rest to his buddies. They cinched loose slacks with belts and gratefully accepted the shirts and jackets.

Grandfather asked the family's housekeeper to make Dad's favorite dishes, but for the first time in his life Dad had no appetite. He stared at the arrangement of food in front of him without pleasure. At the end of the meal with his parents, he bid them farewell with a heavy heart and headed home to his young family.

IN THE IMMEDIATE AFTERMATH of the war, the communists held public executions to deepen fear in the people of South Vietnam. While he waited to report to the detention center, Dad learned of the death of Major Que, an officer in the 16th Regiment. Villagers reported that, before his death, the communists made Major Que dig a hole, large enough to encase his head. Then they tied Major Que's hands and feet together and lowered him headfirst into the hole. They covered the hole with dirt to slowly suffocate him. People could hear him screaming in agony for hours until death silenced him.

The new conquerors sought to change the culture, identity, and way of life of South Vietnam. Saigon was renamed Ho Chi Minh City in honor of their communist leader. They stripped businesses, land, homes, and personal possessions away from private owners. The communist *dong* replaced the South's currency. Money saved in banks became worthless. Everyone lived in poverty postwar. Food became scarce. The communists confiscated meat from vendors to feed their own families and soldiers. The South Vietnamese who sympathized with and helped the communists during the war became outraged when they saw their lives worsen and promises broken in the aftermath.

Angry village women who gave up their sons and daughters to fight for the Viet Cong lamented about how they felt betrayed. Yet they did not dare to publicly denounce or protest against the new government. Freedom of speech no longer existed, and protests resulted in imprisonment. School curricula were changed to teach only communist history and beliefs.

Throughout South Vietnam, the new regime ordered people with connections to the former South Vietnamese government and military, as well as political dissidents, to report to detention centers. From there, they were dispersed to prison camps based on rank and the level of threat. The communists reserved the longest and harshest sentences for the high-ranking general officers or those deemed hardest to reform, whether military or civilian political dissidents. Bribery lessened the sentences. Whatever little gold or precious jewelry people hid from confiscation, they gave to corrupt communist officials to save their imprisoned families. The Bamboo Curtain had fallen on all of Vietnam.

AFTER THREE DAYS HOME, in the first week of May 1975 Dad heard the announcement over the radio and megaphones attached to electrical poles throughout town instructing all military and government personnel to report to the city jail. Approximately four hundred people from different ranks and branches showed up to the old building constructed during the French colonial days to imprison criminals. The city jail served as a temporary stop, used to sort the detainees into the jungle prisons waiting throughout Vietnam.

The communists rounded the prisoners into the open-jail cafeteria and divided them into groups of twenty. The guards assigned the lowest ranking member in the group to be the leader, thus initiating their mind games and inflicting humiliation. Dad, being the most junior ranked in his group, became the leader to a team of colonels. The guards instructed Dad to give his superiors orders to sweep the jail. The men understood the tactics being played and kept their cool. When Dad took a broom to help, the guard pulled the broom from his hand and struck it across his back. Dad felt the sharp sting along his spine and the impulse to pummel the guard. But the other prisoners gave him a sharp look to remain calm.

Before the communists shipped him out to the jungle prison camp, Dad received news from his mother who was allowed a brief jail visit. She wept and told him, "Your father was imprisoned with a crowd of townspeople and business owners. The communists took our brick factory."

Grandfather Luong was unaware that while the new authorities interrogated and forced him to write confessions, hundreds of villagers, whose lives benefited from the brick factory, started a petition to free him. Even villagers who helped the Viet Cong during the war used their influence to clear him. They wrote letters vouching for his fairness and honesty. After two months of steady petitions from the citizens of Vinh Long, the communists released Grandfather.

Dad also learned that they sentenced Mom, along with other officers' wives, to till farmland with shovels and picks every day for six months as punishment for their husbands' "crimes." Dad wanted to take the same shovel and clobber the new regime when he heard the news.

CHAPTER 13

The Second Imprisonment

GENERAL DI SETTLED INTO a corner of the small shed-turned-prison-cell alongside twenty-nine other generals at the Quang Trung National Training Center. After several months at Can Tho, guards moved General Di to Quang Trung. He became a prisoner at the center he once commanded.

Each general had just enough room to lie in the fetal position, side by side. With no pillow or blanket and just the clothes on his back to cushion him from the musty hard floor, General Di lay down and said a silent prayer. He prayed for his family, his friends, and his soldiers. He did not know their fate, and they did not know his. He only knew, on that night of May 1975, that he was in the Hoc Mon District of Saigon, still in South Vietnam.

The early days of incarceration involved fifteen minutes of physical exercise in the morning, followed by four hours of "reeducation training," a lunch consisting of a small bowl of rice with dried anchovy, then another four hours of "reeducation." Dinner followed, with the same diet as lunch and breakfast.

"You are the enemy of the people and the henchmen lackeys of US imperialism. Marxism and Leninism will prevail and bury capitalism," the communist instructors drilled into the prisoners.

General Di thought to himself: *This is not reeducation, it is brainwashing.* He felt disgusted with himself for repeating the lies the communists forced him to say and write. Guilt and shame gnawed at him every time they made him ask for "leniency from the people and the Revolutionary Government."

I shamed my country, the Republic of Vietnam. I dishonored my army, his thoughts painfully tormented him. But he had to stay alive for his family. To survive and to keep from breaking under the psychological torture, he built a wall around his heart and mind.

Foreign delegations such as the Red Cross and Amnesty International tried to monitor the conditions of the prison camps. However, they never got to see the true conditions. Prisoners were forced to memorize scripts written by the communists to report to visitors. The guards took internees deemed not reformed into the jungles to hide them until the delegates left.

On April 30, 1976, at the one-year anniversary of South Vietnam's surrender, General Di found himself sitting on a stool with a bucket of fish in the prison courtyard while photographers from *Time, Newsweek*, and the French press shot pictures. The communists invited the international press to the prison for a staged photo opportunity to show the world that the prisoners were alive and doing well.

A nearby team of communist officials directed General Di to scale the fish. He stared at the bucket in front of him with a detached look. When a reporter attempted to ask him a question, General Di remembered the warning given by the prison authorities not to engage with the press. When the reporter persisted, a guard intervened and pulled General Di away. After the press left, the guards removed the props. General Di ate stale rice without fish that evening.

The next night, guards came to his cell and placed shackles on General Di's ankles and cuffed his hands. They shoved him into a cargo truck with a group of generals and field grade officers and drove them to an airfield where a military plane waited. He recognized the plane as one that had belonged to the South Vietnamese military fleet, and the pilots were former South Vietnamese military pilots. The communist regime did not have enough planes or trained pilots for the large-scale exile they planned.

The mass deportation of 1976 resulted in the removal from South Vietnam of thousands of former government, military, police, and political dissidents from temporary camps in the South to remote prisons in the mountainous regions of North Vietnam. The communist regime labeled this group as posing the greatest threat and, therefore, required the harshest sentence. This move marked the true punishment phase.

The plane flew to North Vietnam where the mountains with thick forests of evergreen trees replaced the tropical lowlands and mangroves of the Mekong Delta. After June 1976, General Di was moved to a series of prisons from Yen Bai to Ha Tay, Nam Ha, and finally Ham Tan prison. He was kept on the move so that his status and location became elusive and hard to track for his family and human rights organizations.

LAYER UPON LAYER OF branches woven with vines allowed only a few streaks of sunlight to pierce through the dark, highland jungle. In this hidden locale, General Di heard birds cawing and the hollering of guards ordering prisoners to chop trees to build their shelters at the prison camp in Yen Bai. Nothing but evergreen trees, patches of palms, and hanging vines surrounded him—no man-made structures were in sight.

The guards handed out machetes and axes while firmly holding their rifles. General Di joined his fellow prisoners to clear the dense jungle. They chopped trees and vines to assemble crude shelters. They learned to build without nails, using vines and thinly sheared bamboo trees to bind the logs and limbs that formed the walls and roofs together. After they built shelters, they dug wells and planted cassava roots. At the end of the long day of back-breaking labor, they received one small bowl of rice.

In the evenings, the internees gathered for political "reeducation." General Di sat on the ground with a group of prisoners while mosquitoes swarmed around them. Lit torches illuminated the communist camp commander who stood in his military uniform with bare feet. The commander started his rant by accusing the inmates of betraying the people of Vietnam. "You were fools! You were exploited by the US. The benevolence of the new communist government spared your lives." The chastisement went on for hours and ended with the internees repeating what they had learned back to their captors.

The guards then handed out paper and pen for forced confessions. The prisoners had to repent their misdeeds to the satisfaction of the communist officials. The confessions ranged from forced lies to trivial accounts of their lives like listing how many radios and televisions they owned. The communists used the written confessions as justification to the world that the internees had admitted to wrongful deeds and deserved to be punished.

General Di looked at the document he had written with revulsion but concealed his contempt with an aloof look. The instructor, who had no more than an elementary school education, read the confession, then tore it up. "Write it again," he ordered. The prisoners had to write confessions several times over to the satisfaction of their jailer. If the details did not match, they were whipped. The mental thrashing stretched late into the night. On some nights, the guard woke them from sleep and made them bow to the communist cadre who continued hurling insults and accusations at them. Before they could go back to their shelter, they all had to repeat in unison, "We are guilty."

When they forced General Di to write a report on US military strategies, he refused. The camp commander gave him a few minutes to reconsider before he faced punishment. General Di confronted the possibilities of having his fingernails ripped with pliers, being hung from the ceiling and whipped, or locked in a metal Conex box: all popular torture techniques used by the communists.

The camp commander asked again, "Are you ready to write the report?"

General Di answered, "No."

"Take him away," the commander ordered.

They shoved him into a crude bamboo shack about one hundred yards away from the prison barracks. The authorities designated this structure for solitary confinement and prohibited the other prisoners from coming near the enclosure. The thatched-roof and dirt-floor cell had just enough space for him to take a few steps and lay lengthwise on the ground. The guards shut the door and left him standing in semi-darkness. The cracks and crevices of the bamboo walls allowed in stabs of sunlight and air. Still, he felt suffocated by the heat of the noontime sun. The stench of human excrement left behind from previous internees exiled in the bamboo cell overpowered him.

A portion of rice, the size of a teacup, and water mixed with salt sustained him for the day. The salt made him thirsty and sent his innards into knots. Every day for a month, he stared into dull darkness mingled with streaks of light that seeped through. He felt like a caged animal. He prayed to keep his mind from breaking. He asked God to let him make it through another day so that he could be reunited with his family.

After a month, he was released. He placed his hands over his eyes from the burst of punching sunlight when he made his way out of the bamboo cell. But he was relieved to be again in the company of his fellow prisoners. He figured his captors wanted to torture him enough to break him but not enough to kill him. The communists needed to keep the generals alive to use as bargaining chips with the international communities.

WITH A STICK IN one hand and eyes scanning the forest floor, General Di foraged the jungle for a meal. The bowl of rice given each day in the first three months of arrival had ceased to be offered. The detainees had to scavenge for food and wait until the planted cassava roots matured before they could have a small, but steady, supply of food. General Di's eyes stayed alert for frogs, lizards, and insects that hopped and slithered along the jungle floor.

The prisoners eyed the crop of cassava eagerly, waiting until it could be harvested. But the starchy roots that clung together like a cluster of sweet potatoes carried little nutrition. When the roots were ready to be pulled from the soil, hungry prisoners, unfamiliar with the cyanide in the raw plants, ate the roots without properly boiling them. The cassava roots claimed their first victims in the young, inexperienced South Vietnamese officers as the toxin caused them to vomit, collapse, and die shortly afterward. General Di sadly mused that even the food became a cruel trap.

The absence of food was a constant concern for the political inmates. They received meat on four occasions of the year: the first day of the year, three days of the Lunar New Year, May 1, and September 2 to commemorate the communist holidays. They lined up to receive chunks of discarded pork lard. Still, it was just enough meat to tantalize them with what they once had.

Starvation weakened their bodies and their immune systems. It left them vulnerable to diseases like malaria, tuberculosis, and dysentery. Confined quarters and the resultant filth facilitated the rapid transmission of diseases. In many cases, when a prisoner died during imprisonment, the families were never notified.

Imprisoned South Vietnamese military doctors tried to help their fellow internees, but their pleas for treatment of the critically ill frequently went ignored by the guards. The doctors incarcerated with General Di often turned to him for help. Without pause, he approached the prison officials and urged them to allow the sick to get care at a hospital outside of camp. After his having spent several years in North Vietnam's prison, even the communist authorities developed a respect for General Di's character. They relented and allowed sick prisoners to be treated in the hospital.

When the cold mountain air of the early morning came in, it pierced through General Di's tattered clothes and chilled his bones. Each inhalation of cold air narrowed his airway. It caused him to go into coughing fits, gasping for air. The childhood asthma that lay dormant for many years made its return. The captives who witnessed his struggle asked their families who were able to travel to the isolated prison camp to bring in ginger root, a staple in Vietnamese home remedies for curing a variety of illnesses. Even though the inmates' status and location were kept hidden, word eventually reached a few families of the whereabouts of their captured loved ones from released prisoners in the same internment camp. The prisoners shared their precious stash of ginger with General Di, who boiled it and drank it as a tea. The warm spice opened his airway and calmed his stomach.

The ginger remedy did more good than the unknown pills that the communists dispensed to sick internees. For seventeen years, General Di received a pill the prison handed out called *xuyen tam lien*, which meant "heart of lotus," for every complaint. No one knew its indications. He received the same pill regardless of ailment, even if it did not help.

When disease and illness went neglected, the captives turned to their faith in God for comfort. General Di and a group of prisoners gathered at night to pray in secret. General Di prayed, "God, please give us the strength and courage to withstand this suffering."

The prison officials did not allow religious practice of any sort. Atheism was the official creed of the communist party. If caught, the prisoners faced the litany of punishments designed to maim and kill, just as during the war when the communists stabbed chopsticks into the ears or tore the ears partially off with pliers and left them dangling for listening to the Lord's Prayer. This was the penalty for Catholics living in the province of Bao Lac, near the frontier of China.

AS ONE YEAR OF imprisonment dragged to five, cement buildings built by the hands of the prisoners replaced the wood and straw prison barracks. General

Di saw a steady stream of prisoners released while he remained. One constant by General Di's side throughout the seventeen years was his cellmate, Major General Le Minh Dao, the feisty commander of the ARVN's 18th Infantry Division. General Dao stood at average height and build, with dark round eyes, but the spunk and grit that he exuded made him appear twice his stature.

During the war, the two generals had occasionally met at staff meetings. Before 1975, General Dao knew of General Di only in passing and what he heard from officers in the corps. They described General Di as a disciplined and clean commander who stayed away from bribes and corruption.

Nearing the final days of war, South Vietnamese Vice President Nguyen Cao Ky asked General Dao to help stage a coup against President Nguyen Van Thieu. General Dao responded to Ky, "Too busy fighting the communists. Cannot participate" Like General Di, he stayed away from the political infighting.

In the last month of war, when the communist NVA decimated much of South Vietnam's forces, General Dao's 18th Infantry Division, under assault and outnumbered by four communist divisions, annihilated three of the attacking divisions. Under his spirited command, General Dao's soldiers kept fighting and became one of the last divisions to surrender.

General Dao had the good fortune of a large network of family in Vietnam and abroad. They found ways to track his locations and trekked to each remote prison to bring comfort and news from home. The small but frequent rations that he shared with fellow prisoners sustained them through the years.

General Dao took the pair of blue Levi's jeans and several bars of soap his family brought for him and gave them to the guard. Hidden inside the goods, he tucked a letter written by General Di addressed to his parents in My

Tho. The communist authorities restricted letter writing. Nonetheless, the guard agreed to sneak the letter out in exchange for the coveted pair of jeans and soap.

Somewhere between Hanoi and Saigon's postal route, the courier was intercepted, and General Di's letter was discovered. The prison authorities summoned General Di from his cell and interrogated him for half a day. General Di refused to give up the source that allowed him to smuggle his letter out. When they could not extract any information from him, the guards threw General Di into a separate cell. They confined General Di to a room next to the one that he shared with General Dao. A thin wall that did not go all the way to the ceiling separated them.

When the guards weren't looking, General Dao pressed one side of his face and ear to the wall and whispered, "Brother Di, have they fed you?"

"No, but I am fine. Do not worry," General Di answered. They tried to starve him in the first few days but kept him alive with a few cups of water each day.

"When the guards leave, I will pass food over to you," General Dao said.

General Dao packed his ration of rice tightly together and wrapped it in a bundle. He found a pole and tied the bundle to its tip. He took one last look to make sure that the guards were out of sight then climbed onto a chair in his cell and reached over the wall with the pole to deliver bundles of food to General Di. After a month of solitary confinement, the prison officials were surprised to see General Di in better shape than they expected. They released him back to his cellmates.

"Thank you, Brother. You took a huge risk to save me," General Di said to his friend. He knew that if the guards had caught General Dao smuggling food, his friend would receive a far stiffer punishment than he had himself.

"We are brothers and must always be strong and stand up when the enemy want us to cower," General Dao said to his cellmates.

To annoy the prison guards, General Dao often laughed loudly from his cell even when he felt like crying. He knew that his captors wanted to break their spirits and hated the sound of their laughter. When his cellmates felt down, he reminded them, "When everything is taken away from you, no one can take away your dignity if you decide not to surrender it. When you cannot trust anyone, you have to find a higher power to trust."

CHAPTER 14
Prison Camp

DUSK FADED INTO NIGHTTIME and our car headlights illuminated the highway that crossed through the Florida Everglades. From the road, only a few small shallow marshes could be seen running parallel along the interstate. The clumps of familiar mangroves sprouted from the swamp water.

"This area is a little eerie at night," Mom said. The swampy terrain reminded her of the jungle prison where Dad was held.

"IF YOU DO NOT cooperate, we will kill you all. We will cover it up as a prison escape and no one will know," the camp commander welcomed Dad and his group of nine hundred political inmates to Bau Sen Camp in May 1975.

Plucked from the detention center in Vinh Long, Dad found himself thrown into the jungles of Tra Vinh Province, at the southern coast of Vietnam. The prison site sat five miles from the coast in a low-lying area. Nothing but mangroves, palms, vines, and a few clusters of banana trees enveloped him. Dad and the troop of nine hundred had to build their own prison.

The gnarled mangrove trees with their skinny trunks and tangled web of twiggy roots were interwoven with palms of all sizes. Dad noticed a few small crabs scurry under the tree canopy. High tide from the nearby coast came in and flooded the campground, leaving behind a quagmire of ankle-deep water. Dad detected the damp rotting odor of decaying leaves in the wet mud all around.

On the day of arrival, his eyes scanned the camp looking for a break that might allow an escape. But Dad reasoned that his chance of surviving was low when he considered guards with rifles loaded and ready to shoot any escapees. If he did make it past the guards, he had to find his way out of a dark jungle saturated with Viet Cong booby traps waiting to mutilate and leave him dying alone. If by a slim chance he made it out of the wilderness, he would encounter villages of hostile Viet Cong sympathizers ready to report him. By design, the communists positioned the prison camps near secluded villages that supported them during the war. The jungle turned into one giant prison cell.

The prisoners got to work building their own shelters. Before they could start, they had to clear the area with machetes and dig for soil to elevate the camp foundation. The camp authorities divided them into groups of fifty to construct huts, made with trees they chopped and palm fronds that they piled on top for roofs. Inside the huts, they pounded the earthen floor to an even smooth surface.

In the first few months they slept on the ground with mats made from banana leaves. During their breaks, they constructed cots, three feet wide and five feet long, from tree branches and twigs tied together. They built a row of nineteen huts with fifty men in each, with a two-foot space between each cot.

After the huts, three guard shacks went up. One guard shack stood at the end of the hut barracks and one in the camp's front entrance. While the prisoners worked, fifty armed guards kept watch.

THE BUMPS AND RIPPLES of his tree bed poked against Dad's spine and shoulder, making sleep difficult. Outside, the owls, frogs, and crickets sang their nightly songs, and inside the sound of snores and growling stomachs joined the chorus. Dad stayed awake, thinking of home.

He thought about the first time he had held his first born, a son he named Van. The tiny infant fell asleep curled in the crook of his arm. The new life he held then felt delicate and innocent, so different from the hardened realities of war around him. He had looked at his sleeping son and wondered if he could be the kind of man his father had been to him. He had the same worries Grandfather Luong had as a new father. Would his son face the cruelty of war?

Suddenly, Dad felt older than his twenty-seven years, yet at times he still felt like a kid. A year after Van came, my parents welcomed me. Dad couldn't go home for my birth. He missed the first birthday and first steps, a luxury known to few fathers who fought in the war. His thoughts returned to Mom, and he worried how she managed alone with two babies under the new regime. He wondered if he would ever return home.

The gnawing pain in his stomach shifted Dad's thoughts to food. That day, the only thing he had eaten had been a small bowl of rice and jungle greens that he boiled. After a day of hard labor, the men received one cup of rice to cook. The guards gave them thirty minutes to scavenge the jungle for additional food. Catching anything that moved became a method to add to the meager bowl of rice. They hunted turtles, jungle rats, snakes, and gathered wild edible plants. Prisoners familiar with jungle vegetation taught other inmates which plants were safe to eat.

In the evenings, the men sat in formation outside the barracks listening to hours of lectures about their evil and misguided actions during the war. The political indoctrination served as their "reeducation." Anyone who spoke up received a beating, had their prison sentence extended, or were even killed.

Dad sat on the ground, listening to the rant. His eyelids became heavy after a long day of arduous labor. Just before he closed his eyes to doze off, one of the inmates tapped his arm and warned, "Wake up! They'll give you a beating if they catch you sleeping."

Dad replied, "I was never a good student. Why start now?"

A guard heard him and took the butt of an AK-47 and struck it against Dad's shoulder.

In the first three months of his imprisonment, each night before he went to sleep a guard shackled one of Dad's ankles with that of another prisoner and so on down a line to form a twelve-man link of prisoners to prevent them from escaping. In the first month, the heavy metal cuffs bore into Dad's ankle, creating a red sore. By the end of the third month, his bones stuck out as the protective padding from his muscles and fat shriveled away. The clothes hung loose on his shrinking frame while the shackles slid off his ankle and foot.

In the morning, the guards removed the shackles. In groups of several hundreds, the prisoners walked toward the coast to brush their teeth with salt water. The toothbrushes, brought from home, had to last for the duration of an unknown prison sentence.

Dad tasted the sea as he swished the salt water in his mouth. It made him thirsty, but he would have to wait until after the walk back to camp to drink well water. He washed his face and neck to rinse off the dirt and grime from the previous day's work. The salt water stung the itchy red patch of ringworm that expanded from his armpit to his chest. He noticed that some of the men had the same rash. Others had angry red bumps from infected bites of jungle insects. They scratched and picked at their sores for relief. The constant sticky heat made the itching and infections worse.

When they got back to camp, the inmates separated into work units for different labor assignments for the day. While one group cleared the jungle, another group scooped fish and shrimp that flowed inland with the high tide. The men could not eat the catch. The prison officials collected the baskets of seafood and shipped them off for sale.

CHAPTER 15

Survival

DAD FOLLOWED HIS WORK group to a jungle clearing one mile from camp. The month before, he and several hundred men were ordered to clear a piece of land that spanned three miles long and one mile wide. They dug down a foot over part of the area, creating a gouge that turned into a shallow pond when the tide rose and filled the hole. They used the extracted soil to build elevated roads for the surrounding villages. The tidewater brought in aquatic life from the gulf that filled the pond. The prison authorities found an opportunity to make money and ordered the prisoners to fish and shrimp during high tide.

While the men worked, the communist cadre shouted, "Repent through labor!"

Dad waded through the knee-high muddy water and stepped into a spot that dropped him a foot deeper. He stumbled into one of many craters scattered throughout the man-made pond that incoming bombs had created during the war. The sea creatures favored the craters and collected inside its pockets. Dad took his net and sifted the water. He scooped a handful of plump shrimp into his net. They joggled inside the net, looking fresh and tempting.

Dad's empty stomach battled with his brain—should he take a risk to satisfy his hunger and suffer a beating if caught? When he saw the guards look away, he devoured one shrimp still wiggling in its translucent shell. The sweet slippery flesh and the crunch from the shell slid quickly down his throat. He savored the briny aftertaste and snuck a couple more crustaceans into his pockets for his evening meal. The other prisoners followed suit and cautiously filled their own pockets. As the months progressed, the prisoners shrimped and fished so much that their efforts eventually depleted the region's supply. The local villagers who also depended on the water for their livelihood complained to the communist authorities but could do no more.

Despite the steady harvest of seafood, the prison officials wanted a bigger catch. They wanted the men to drain the surrounding rivers with a dam. The camp commander ordered the internees to build a forty-foot-high dam using tree limbs for the skeleton and mud for the filler. The men voiced concerns to each other about the dangerous plan.

Nonetheless, two hundred workers, including Dad, toiled under the hot sun to complete the structure. While he dug mud with his bare hands, Dad heard the guards taunt, "Labor is glory! Labor is glory!" He wanted to throw a handful of mud at their faces. He wondered how much glory they would find in forced labor, feeling their backs ache and their bellies hurt.

Halfway through the project, while Dad and the other prisoners covered the dam with river mud, they heard popping and snapping sounds. Then someone screamed, "Get out of the river!"

A torrent of water crashed through the dam. The water pressure from high tide snapped the dam's wooden skeleton. Dad bolted for the riverbank and pulled himself out of the water just in time. Everyone dashed out of the river and survived the devastating rush of water.

When the prisoners worked outside of camp, they were housed with villagers. The prison officials ordered the villagers to share their homes with the internees. The men usually slept under outdoor coverings or inside sheds. More freedom and fewer restrictions outside of the camp temporarily eased the prisoners' suffering. The men could fish the rivers and ponds on their own after work. On some lucky evenings, they caught enough food to share with their hosts, many of whom did not have enough to eat.

Over time, the villagers got to know the political inmates, and their perceptions changed. Before the men entered prison camp, the officials warned villagers that the prisoners were vile and not to be trusted. The locals believed them, as they had only heard the Viet Cong propaganda during the war. On one occasion, an elderly village man came to Dad and admitted, "Now that we know you men firsthand, you aren't bad at all. We feel sorry for you. Most of you are still young, educated, and now you are subjected to such a hard life."

Dad even shared a meal with one former North Vietnamese soldier who had retired from the NVA due to a war injury. The NVA soldier returned to live in his hamlet to farm with his wife and daughter. At the end of the workday, he invited Dad into his home for supper. Never one to turn down a meal and a drink, Dad accepted. For both sides, the simple meal offered the chance to understand the human side of war once they met and learned about an enemy soldier who held no gun.

The NVA soldier said to Dad, "If you did not kill me during the war, I would kill you. That is war. But in the end, we are all human."

Dad nodded. But he knew that for many, on both sides, the division and animosity remained deep.

MOST OF THE GUARD were teenagers. They yelled and screamed orders to men twice their age. Yet, Dad discovered that some, still boys, had not turned mean or been jaded by war. He knew the teenage guards listened to their conversations at night when the men lay in their cots and talked about their families and the food they would enjoy once released.

For entertainment, some of the better storytellers told tales of Vietnamese folklore, of adventures, and of battles with heroes and villains. They knew some of the young guards often gathered outside the hut to secretly listen. Their best storyteller decided to play a joke one night. He told an epic tale with such zeal that his audience listened spellbound. When he got to the cliffhanger, he pretended to yawn and told everyone he was going to sleep. The prisoners heard the guards from outside protest, "Hey, finish the story!"

On most evenings, the internees' thoughts turned to home. Dad made a new friend, Em, who hailed from the same hometown. Em flew gunship helicopters for the ARVN units. He clocked in three thousand miles and survived two crashes from enemy fire during the war. On the second crash, he cracked his skull and broke his leg. Still, he returned to action after two months. One night, Em told Dad and several other prisoners about his new bride and his elderly mother at home. He came from a poor family. His sister, a schoolteacher, sold noodles at a food stall for extra money to support their mother.

Em shared his story with Dad and the curious prisoners, who wondered if he tried to escape the communists with his helicopter on the day of surrender. They listened intently to Em as he recalled flying a chopper packed with evacuees on April 30, 1975, to the island of Phu Quoc, off the southern tip of Vietnam. He told them that a fleet of

American battleships waited along the coast. He couldn't land his chopper on the ships due to the limited space needed for the returning US aircraft. He landed instead on Phu Quoc Island. From there, the escapees boarded fishing boats to get to the awaiting armada He could have joined them but sat in the chopper. The image of his mother and young wife tugged at his heart. He was at a crossroads—escape and leave his loved ones behind or return for them. He couldn't abandon them. Em turned the chopper around and flew back.

"And here you are with us. Big dummy!" Dad teased. But he understood.

When the men entered prison camp, they could only bring in one extra pair of clothes to last them for an unknown number of years. By the end of the second year, Dad's two pairs of trousers and both shirts had thinned and faded from constant wear and taxing labor. He didn't worry about his clothes, but some of the other prisoners with the same torn and tattered clothes had an idea when they spotted sandbags left behind after the war in the villages. They emptied the bags and used the fabrics to make shorts and shirts. The soiled and ragged sandbag fabric weathered much better than their own clothes. With the needles and threads that their families snuck in during prison visits, they made new sets of clothes. Some of the prisoners who had a talent for sewing made a complete outfit from two or three empty sandbags.

Dad declined the offer for a sandbag outfit. Instead, he accepted a lunch bag that a fellow internee, with extra fabric, made for him. When the communists honored their founding leader, Ho Chi Minh, on a national holiday, the prisoners dug out their sandbag outfit and as an inside joke wore it in "honor" of "Uncle Ho." It was a silent protest among the men to mark their miserable state thanks to Ho Chi Minh.

Trees, heavy with green and yellow clusters of banana-like plantain fruits, encircled the camp. The prisoners were not allowed to eat the plantains, while the guards would eat only half and throw the rest away. Dad and the other inmates hungrily surveyed the trees with their tempting fruits, glistening from the monsoon rain. One night, when the guards tucked themselves inside their dry shelter, Dad and two other prisoners decided to sneak out of their hut, into the rain, to pick the plantains they had been eyeing for some time. The targeted tree stood about thirty yards from their hut. Dad volunteered to be the lookout, while the other two snatched the fruit. One man sat on the shoulder of another man to reach the bunch. They had a small knife that they used to hack away the stem of the fruit cluster. Dad kept watch while his hand swatted mosquitoes that swarmed around his neck and arms.

They snuck back with each man carrying a cluster of green plantains. They gave two plantains to whoever was awake. The large green plantains needed to be boiled to get the best taste. Another conspirator waited with a pot of boiling water. The fruit needed several minutes to cook. Dad pulled the cooked brown peels off, stopping only to blow on the tips of his burnt fingers. He bit into the starchy plantain with steam still coming from it. He devoured the plantain despite a burnt tongue. The taste and smell reminded him of a potato. But most of all, the familiar taste brought him home. After the men ate, they buried the peels in a corner of the hut.

The next morning, Dad woke up with a slight belly ache, fever, and chills. He blamed it on indigestion from the green plantain. He pushed through the day until he felt dizzy and started shaking. A fellow prisoner who had completed two years of medical school diagnosed Dad with malaria. He told Dad to get treated at the prison clinic. A guard walked him to a bamboo shack two miles outside of camp where a communist "doctor" saw him. The practitioner, with no more than an elementary school education, pointed his finger at Dad and hollered, "What do you want?"

Dad described his symptoms: "I feel hot and cold all at once. My body aches and . . ."

The "doctor" stopped him before he could finish. He then opened a book. He studied the page and, with his finger, went down a list of symptoms that matched. Then he ran his fingers across the page to find the matching treatment. Without performing a physical exam, he gave Dad a handful of chloroquine pills.

The prison clinic dispensed chloroquine for almost every ailment—whether cold, rash, or belly ache. The communists treated prisoners with the remaining medicine that they had confiscated from the South Vietnamese military. The south had an abundant supply of chloroquine, due to the prevalence of malaria in Southeast Asia.

Dental care was not much better. When Dad had a toothache, a guard took him outside of camp to visit the village dentist, a farmer who practiced dentistry part-time. The dentist, a former communist soldier, had injured his left arm during the war, leaving it contracted. He held the wounded arm close to his body. A shed served as an office where the dentist stored his farm tools and dental supplies. The dental equipment consisted of a pair of rusty pliers, an unidentified purple liquid in a bottle, some needles, and a few cotton balls.

The dentist came in from the field soaking with sweat. He reeked of manure. He leaned toward Dad, who sat on a simple wooden stool that served as the dental chair. The dentist poked at the tooth for a few seconds and offered to pull it. Dad wanted to bolt out of the chair, but he was in so much pain already that he couldn't imagine it being worse.

"Let me numb the area first," the dentist offered. He injected the purple liquid into Dad's gum.

"Ahhh!" Dad screamed when the dentist gave a tug on the tooth, but his pain went ignored.

The dentist held the pliers with his good arm and steadied the bad arm against Dad's chest. He yanked harder, and Dad screamed louder. He tugged again, but the tooth would not budge. On the third try, he lost his grip and dropped the pliers to the ground. He picked up the pliers and continued to pull. With each tug, Dad thought he would lose control of his bladder.

"Stop squirming!" the dentist ordered.

On the final attempt, the dentist placed his bad arm against the front center of Dad's neck to get a firmer hold. He didn't seem to care that his arm blocked Dad's airway. With his good arm, he gave a strong yank, which caused Dad to shoot out of his chair and the tooth to fly out of his mouth.

Dad sat down drenched in perspiration, heart racing, and spat out a mouthful of blood while holding his throbbing head.

The dentist held up Dad's tooth and examined the long root. "That'll be ten dollars," he said.

Dad held the side of his swollen jaw with one hand and reached into his pocket with the other to pull out the money that Mom had given him on her last visit. *Nothing came free—not even agony*, Dad thought.

When he got back to camp, he swished his swollen mouth with salt water. He had no medicine to numb the pain, just salt to provide a little antiseptic. He held the salt water inside his mouth for the rest of the evening to prevent infection.

During Dad's imprisonment, Mom would sometimes make the long venture to visit him. The travel required multiple stops and transfers on unreliable vehicles and hazardous roads. Often, the only transportation available was rusty French minibuses built in the 1940s. Such a minibus could fit fourteen passengers, but around thirty squeezed inside, with a dozen more sitting on the roof, holding on to the two metal rails welded on top. The last bus stopped at the town of Tra Vinh. From there, Mom made her way on foot through the jungle. Sometimes she found a local who helped her with directions, but most of the time the communist loyalists gave her a harsh, disdainful look without offering any help.

On one visit, Mom carried two parcels in her arms containing dried fish, fruit, a bottle of medicine for abdominal ailments, and a pair of trousers she had sewn for Dad. After the war, among other survival skills, she had learned to sew and cook.

Dusk arrived. Light slipped away fast, leaving total darkness without any sign of civilization in the forbidding jungle. Mom had not planned to arrive late, but on her ride to Tra Vinh, the bus in front of her vehicle hit a land mine that blasted away a section of the road. She and her fellow passengers got out of their intact bus and cleared away chunks of concrete. The male passengers pushed the charred bus clear of the path. Mom didn't want to look at the disfigured bodies that were laid at the side of the road.

Later on, alone in the dark, Mom felt her palms and forehead dripping with sweat from fear and physical exhaustion, yet she pushed through the jungle, not sure of where she was going. Total darkness enveloped her, and she could barely see her hands in front of her face. She prayed and cried as she ran forward. She faced lurking dangers, such as remnants of Viet Cong traps, deadly snakes, spiders, and wild boars. She thought about my brother and me, waiting at home, and wanted to return to us.

Sharp twigs and thorns scratched her face and arms as she barreled through the trail. Her feet tripped over the gnarled root of a mangrove tree that sent her crashing, face forward, hitting the jungle floor. She heard the whistles and croaks of birds and lizards, seeming to taunt her while she sat rubbing her ankle that had twisted in the tree root. She brushed the dirt and sweat off her face and limped ahead. She heard the sound of running water from a narrow stream and followed it until she saw the glow of kerosene lamps coming from a cluster of homes.

Mom knocked on the door of a house that belonged to an elderly couple. At first, they looked at her with distrust, but when they noted the scratches across her face and sweat pouring down her forehead, their expressions softened. They allowed Mom to rest in a corner of their home for the night. In the morning, they pointed her in the direction of the camp. She arrived at the front guard shack with her two parcels, which the guards rummaged through. They told Mom, "You brought too much." They confiscated one package of food and gave the rest back. They called Dad to the guard shack for the supervised visit.

Dad saw the tired look in Mom's eyes and her hollow cheeks. She told him about Van and me but did not have any pictures to show him. She barely had enough money each month to feed us. When the fifteen-minute visit ended, the guards sent Mom away. Every four months she made the perilous journey again to bring a little comfort from home, all the while enduring misery and doing without.

Marriage, war, the births of children, the death of her beloved mother, followed by Dad's imprisonment, within quick succession, changed life for Mom. All this happened before she had turned twenty-five. The days of protection and pampering from her parents were long gone. She raised her children alone, not knowing the fate of her husband.

My brother Van and I lived in a small cement building with Mom on a property that belonged to Grandfather Luong. A wide gravel yard surrounded the front, where a few commercial buses parked. Behind our house and beyond the parking lot, a sprawling field of wild vegetation surrounded us.

On some mornings, Mom started her daily chores by shearing the tall grass with an old farm sickle. She moved through the pasture, clipping the thick vegetation with two piglets trailing behind her. After the purchase of her two piglets, she did not have money left for animal feed. She prayed that her pigs would not get sick eating the grass and foliage. It was all that she could offer them. Mom knew nothing about raising pigs, but she hoped to sell her hogs for at least a modest price and perhaps raise more swine. With two filled bags of greens, she walked back to the pen with her pigs.

During those solitary walks, Mom thought about her mother who had died a year before Dad was imprisoned. Her gentle mother, who never raised her voice or had a mean word for anyone, passed away suddenly at age fifty-eight. Grandmother Thao took ill with fever one day but reassured her family that she would be fine when they wanted to take her to the doctor in town. She did not want to burden them with the cost of treatment when she saw how they lived in deprivation since the communist take-over. Grandmother Thao passed away in her sleep a few nights after her symptoms first appeared. Mom was devastated when she heard the news. In the days and weeks following her mother's death, Mom could not find the strength to get out of bed, but she had to muster the will to continue.

The wet nudge against her ankle from the pink snout of her two piglets temporarily broke her sorrows. Their squeals and oinks tempered her loneliness. The little animals followed Mom around and kept her company, like pets, as she did her chores.

DAD SAT IN THE dirt courtyard in front of the barrack hut, in the same spot he had sat over the past three years alongside the other hundreds of political inmates when they were called to gather either for chastisement or for release. He saw the size of the camp gradually dwindle as prisoners were released in small waves over the years. Release from prison came without any foreknowledge. The prison officials kept the release a secret until the internees heard their names called.

Dad wondered when it would be his turn to go home. He joked to his friends that day in May 1978 that he would be next while they sat listening to the names called out. Near the end of the list, he heard, "Lieutenant Quan, Le, 9th Infantry Division, 16th Regiment."

Dad had a history of being surprised when it involved his name on a list, but this particular shock brought tears of relief. He packed his tattered clothes in one small bundle and walked out of prison. In his mind, he saw himself sprinting out of the front gate.

DAD CHUGGED ALONG ON his father's old farm tractor listening to the droning sound of the engine and smelling diesel mixed with manure as he tilled the soil. Instead of letting him go home to his family, the authorities made him resettle in a rural village an hour away from home to work the land. The only occupation allowed to political prisoners after release was manual labor. Dad knew nothing about farming. Nonetheless, he borrowed a small tractor that Grandfather Luong still owned and, for the next three months, he found work tilling farmland.

Dad mused about how quickly life's fortune changed while the tractor plowed away. One moment, he lived a privileged life being the eldest son in an affluent family. The next, he wore tattered clothes and did not have enough to eat. Worst of all, he had lost his freedom—inside and outside of prison.

The communist officials did not allow him to visit home or travel from one district to the next without permission. The new government enlisted and encouraged informants throughout towns and neighborhoods to report people suspected of breaking the new rules. Regardless, Dad found ways to sneak home on weekends with help from Mom who bribed the local informant with a few dollars and a bag of fruit.

Dad resigned himself to his new livelihood until the communists confiscated the tractor. Without any explanation, they took away his tractor and claimed it as property of the government. Feeling angry and defeated, Dad searched for work. He had few options besides menial labor, despite his education. He knew that while the communists made life difficult for everyone in the South, they intentionally discriminated against political prisoners and their families.

On a secret visit home, Dad sat on a stool next to Mom in the courtyard behind our house, watching my brother and me play with a puppy given to us by my aunt. We named him Marble because he loved to roll on the ground. The little mutt had features of a beagle with swirls of black and brown hair. Even while just a puppy, Marble was smart and protective. He barked at strangers who came to the house and retreated when told to back off. He ate table scraps and, on a few occasions, joined the pigs eating wild vegetation when there was not enough food.

Dad felt helpless that he didn't even have the means to feed the dog. How could he raise a family? Dad admitted to Mom, "There is no future for us and our children here."

Just when he was at his lowest point, Dad received a visit from Grandfather Luong. Dad noticed that the man whom he idolized, who took care of everyone and had a solution for all problems, looked tired. Grandfather's eyes sunk further back behind his glasses, and more lines etched across his face.

"How are you feeling, *Ba*?" Dad asked.

"My diabetes has gotten a little worse. But I will be fine," Grandfather Luong answered with a weary smile. "I am more concerned about you, your family, and your siblings." Dad agreed with his father that living without freedom in communist Vietnam was like a slow and painful exsanguination of the life force that still boiled inside of them all.

"Your mother and I, we are old. But there is still time for the rest of you." Grandfather continued, "I tried to send you out of Vietnam once, but you refused. I am going to give you another opportunity to escape—with your family."

CHAPTER 16

The Escape

"ARE WE STOPPING SOON for the night?" I asked, not sure about Cousin Hung's itinerary. We had covered a good chunk of Florida's western coast and it was getting late by the time we crossed the Everglades. We found a roadside hotel and retired for the night.

Before going to sleep, I replayed the stories that I learned that day in my mind. I felt both respect and sadness for the suffering that my father and General Di had endured through war and its aftermath. At the same time, I saw the lighthearted spirit still strong in both men. Their eyes lit with optimism and the tone of their voices resonated resiliency. They made me feel safe and fortunate.

I thought about how different my life would have turned out if my family had remained in Vietnam. My opportunities for education and military service would not have been possible growing up under the communist regime. I easily saw myself struggling to make a living selling noodles or hawking merchandise on the streets of Saigon, like

so many persecuted families of former South Vietnamese
military members. I became even more grateful to my parents for their courage to flee our native land.

"WE'RE GOING TO A place very far from here,"
Mom told my brother, Van, and me on our last day at home
in Vietnam, in 1978.

"Can I take my dog along?" I asked. I was four and Van
was five at the time.

"Will we see our father?" Van added. She did not tell us
that Grandfather Luong had planned for us to secretly
meet Dad in Saigon where we would obtain fake travel
documents so that we could leave together to the coastal
city of Rach Gia. There, a fishing boat waited to take us and
a group of other escapees out of Vietnam.

Mom stood stoically outside our house, but her stomach
twisted with fear as we waited for the taxi that would take
us into Saigon. She fibbed to neighbors, days before, that
we were approved to visit relatives in the next town. Mom
knew the sight of a car drew the attention of informants
even blocks away.

Marble sat in front of the house, gazing at us as if sensing that something was different that day. Van and I gave
him a last hug and pat on the head. He licked our soft faces
to show his love. When the taxi arrived, he barked nonstop,
trying to frighten it away. Mom signaled at Marble to quiet
down. She felt relief knowing that Grandfather Luong
promised to look after him.

We climbed into the taxi while Marble sat like a stone,
obeying Mom's order. When the taxi sped off, Marble
chased after it. The little dog normally never pursued cars,
but that day he ran like never before. We watched him from
the rear window trying with all his might to keep up with
the taxi. The farther along the road we got, the smaller

Marble became until he disappeared out of sight and out of our lives forever.

LESS THAN A YEAR after Dad's release, in November 1978, my parents made the decision to flee Vietnam. They had to keep their plan a secret, even from family. We fled with over three hundred escapees in a flimsy wooden fishing boat built to hold a maximum of a hundred people. In complete darkness, small groups of people snuck on to the fishing boat until all 340 passengers boarded. The captain set the boat's course for a three-day, three-night voyage to Thailand. One of his crew, a Thai man, knew the region where we would be making port and its dangers.

The captain made repeated trips, smuggling escapees from the coast of Vietnam to Thailand. He had turned the dangerous missions into a lucrative business. The tickets had to be paid in gold. Grandfather Luong provided thirty ounces of gold for our passage. Against Grandfather's wishes, Dad promised to pay back the amount once he reached the west. But first, our boat had to slip past the guards patrolling the coast. If seized, everyone on board— including women and children –would be jailed.

We sat knees bent to our chest, side by side, in the lower deck. My family squeezed together tight, with no room to stretch. Most of the men occupied the outer deck. The enclosed compartment reeked of body odor and vomit, made worse by the humidity. Feeling dizzy from lack of food, little water, and exhaustion, Mom struggled to keep her eyes open. Dad pulled her toward him while Van and I clung to her. Passengers around us did not fare well either. Some fainted, others gagged up saliva and water. But at least we evaded capture by the communists that first night.

On the second day, we crossed into what people called "dark water," which signaled entry into the deep sea. The lone, fragile boat seemed to sail into the abyss without any lifeline. That morning, we encountered rough weather with a brewing storm. The skies darkened. The winds picked up and pushed the wooden boat side to side. The slow, undulating motion started to rock with more force as the waves rose higher and splashed into the boat. The engine stopped. The captain tried to crank it up again, but nothing happened. The engine remained silent. The sea tossed our derelict boat.

Some passengers began praying out loud while others panicked and screamed, "The storm will surely break the boat apart!"

The rocking motion of the fishing boat made Dad nauseated, but he could not relieve the condition with vomiting. His empty stomach churned and growled from having gone two days without food. Dad looked at Van and me clinging to Mom, and he felt worse for us.

A few men on board guessed that the boat's battery had died. They scrambled to look for a sturdy rope to crank the pulley, hoping it would restart the engine. Dad followed them to the front of the boat. They found a cord and wrapped it around the engine's pulley and gave it a yank. On the first attempt, they heard nothing. On the second and third yank, still silence. The sound of prayers became louder, and Dad could hear the desperation in the escapees' voices.

The winds picked up stronger and the skies grew darker. Dad's pulse soared as he braced for the worst. On the fourth try, the engine fired. The putter and roar of the engine was the miraculous sound of survival that gave life back to everyone on board. Some passengers clapped, while others uttered a prayer of gratitude.

The captain raced the boat away from the storm. We were one day closer to land and freedom. By this time, people had become weak and sick from hunger, thirst, and poor sanitation. My lightheadedness came in succession, like the waves bashing against the boat. I could hear the surrounding chatter of the adults, those who still had enough energy, trying to boost everyone's spirits by talking about America and the food we would eat when we arrived at our new home. A man quipped to comfort the crowd, "America is the land of milk and honey and hamburgers!" The talk did not fill our empty bellies, but it fueled our tired spirits with hope.

Late evening of day three, when we were almost to the Thai shore, a wooden motorboat with an angry-looking crew of men pulled alongside us. Their eyes were dull and hungry, as though they had crossed the line of decency without remorse. Dad counted at least forty of them, armed with knives and pistols, ready to pillage. The captain recognized them as Thai pirates. He raced out of the steering cabin, clutching his M16 rifle, and yelled, "All women and children hide below deck!"

He commanded the men on board to surround the boat's outer perimeter. The rest of the passengers on the inside huddled even closer together and prayed harder than before.

Thai pirates trolled the South China Sea and the Gulf of Thailand preying on vulnerable fishing boats packed with escapees during the time of the mass exodus from Vietnam from 1975 to 1995. The pirates often abducted the victims: some they robbed, some they killed, and others they raped. The United Nations High Commissioner for Refugees (UNHCR) compiled statistics that showed for the year 1981, of the 452 boats that arrived in Thailand, 349 had been attacked by pirates, from which "228 women had been abducted; and 881 people were dead or missing."

The captain handed two loaded M16 rifles and one B40 rocket launcher to his crew. Dad stood on the deck and glared at the pirates that he might soon wrestle. He heard the captain order his Thai crew to communicate with the pirates. The Thai crew gave a series of hand signals that the pirates recognized. They decided to negotiate with the captain.

Dad heard the captain yell out, "If you allow us to safely reach shore, I will give you my gold bars. If you want to fight, we are prepared."

The pirates eyed the rifles and rocket launcher. Dad sensed that some level of reasoning replaced their desire to attack. The negotiation, which took several minutes, seemed like an eternity to everyone hidden inside. Van and I clung to Mom, not grasping the possible tragic outcome, but we sensed something dire was happening. The adults feared that death or abduction would follow soon. Many of the escapees whispered prayers over and over, as others whimpered and cried. Dad prayed internally while keeping a stone-cold face, staring down the foe. He prayed that if we were fated to die that day, whatever horror inflicted would happen quickly.

When we felt the boat move, without hearing gunshots or screams, we sat in stunned silence. One of the men from outside came below deck to let us know that the pirates decided not to attack. They agreed to escort our vessel to shore.

We reached the Chanthaburi Province of eastern Thailand on the third night. We learned that the two other boats that sailed out with us on the same night both sank. Dad checked his watch to note the time: ten p.m. He considered with disbelief and gratitude that within three days, we managed to slip past the communists on the coast of Vietnam, revived a dead boat engine to avoid drifting in the South China Sea, sped away from a storm that had the force to shatter the decrepit boat to pieces, and avoided a massacre by Thai pirates.

What was next? Dad wondered.

The Thai police met us at the shore. The policemen wore stern looks. When the pirates saw the police, they fled. The Thai police arrested the fishing boat captain for unlawfully smuggling refugees into the country. He would spend a year in Thai prison. We, as "boat people," a name coined by the international press, became refugees on foreign soil.

Even though we had safely reached land, new trials and dangers emerged. The Thai police rounded everyone up and put us into one warehouse. The police wore uniforms that represented law and order, but their eyes were as emotionless as the pirates' eyes. They had grown tired of the masses of refugees washing up on their shores since 1975. Resentment and disrespect turned criminal. The Thai police forced everyone to remove jewelry and to hand over all valuables. People who disobeyed or moved too slowly felt the knock of rifle butts on their bodies.

Mom pulled off her gold wedding band, the only valuable she had left, and told Dad, "Give me your ring." She took both gold bands and hid them inside her shoes.

CHAPTER 17

Refugee Camp

DAD WAS RELIEVED TO be out of the confines of the warehouse when he walked up the hill overlooking the camp. He searched for a spot to build our new home. He took a deep breath of coastal air and felt better to be out in the open, rather than crowded with hundreds of escapees in the warehouse. One month after our arrival in Thailand, the police took our group to Laem Sing Refugee Camp, five miles from the beach where our boat landed. Approximately two thousand people lived in the overcrowded settlement when we joined. There were no arranged living quarters waiting for us. We had to build our own shelter.

Dad decided on a hillside location that overlooked the campsite to build our hut. Tree stumps dotted the landscape, with a few remaining palms and clusters of young bamboo plants. Prior groups of refugees had stripped the hills once abundant with tropical trees for firewood and shelter, leaving behind large gouges in the land.

From the hilltop, Dad gazed down toward the camp city with its throngs of shacks constructed from newly cut and scavenged wood, with roofs covered by palm fronds and plastic tarps. Clotheslines hung across the front of each shack, and plastic buckets lay scattered in the dirt, waiting for rainwater. The small dwellings were built side by side, some without any walls. A church built from bamboo wood—the cleanest and sturdiest looking structure—stood at the center of camp.

From his view, Dad saw several beaches away from the settlement. One beach had a long wooden bridge from the shore that went out to the water. The bridge led to an outhouse that sat above the waves. He figured it was built by the first group of refugees who settled the camp. The neighboring beach, more secluded, had large dark boulders on the shore surrounded by walls of rocky cliffs. The waves came in and crashed against the rocks like the mass of refugees crashing on foreign shores.

DAD STUDIED THE BUNDLE of bamboo poles he purchased, looking for the four sturdiest to hold the corners of our hut. *I better do a good job*, he thought. He had sold his and Mom's wedding bands and bought materials to build a shelter. He remembered Mom, with tears in her eyes, tenderly polishing their two gold bands before giving them to the Thai merchant. They both agreed to sell their rings so that we could have a safe home located away from the congested encampment.

The rings did not cover the entire building cost of the hut. Mom and Dad tried to bargain with the Thai merchants through the barbed-wire fence that enclosed the

Mom and Dad stand in front of the hut that was our home in the Laem Sing Refugee Camp in Thailand. (Courtesy of Tran B. Quan)

refugee camp. The merchants, who came to the camp daily to do business, would shake their heads and walk away. It was a pretense to drive the bargaining in their favor.

"My brother and I would like to share the cost with you," a man about Dad's age said when he heard the haggling between Dad and some merchants.

"Give us a corner in the hut and we can chip in too," another man offered. A deal was made with two sets of brothers to share the home. The brothers helped Dad carry the bamboo poles and bundle of leaves up the hill to begin construction. Dad thought he was getting handy at building huts. This was his second hut home in four years, even though he grew up in a brick house with modern amenities like indoor plumbing and electricity.

Dad and the brothers—Toan, Chuong, Sang, and Diep—dug holes, each a foot deep, to insert the bamboo columns. Smaller bamboo poles were strapped together to form the hut floor that sat two feet above the ground. They wove palm leaves into the bamboo frames for the three walls and piled more jungle foliage on top of the roof. They left one wall open in place of a door to allow for ventilation. Several hundred yards from our hut, neighboring huts started to pop up with refugees who felt the same need to be away from the hub of activity.

We settled into hut life with the two pairs of brothers. Toan and Chuong fought like cats and dogs. The serious older brother, Toan, relentlessly nagged his rebellious teenage brother. The other pair of brothers, Sang and Diep, settled in their corner, quiet as mice. Sang was a silent man with deep emotions. He missed his wife terribly, and the separation was sometimes unbearable for him. On most days, he sat hunched in a dim corner with pen and paper in hand, crying while composing long love letters to his wife.

One afternoon, the wind blew fiercely and ripped clotheslines off homes, tossing shirts and undergarments across the camp. Buckets and baskets went flying in different directions. The hut protected us from light rain, but we were at the mercy of the mightier storms that turned daytime into night.

We rushed inside the hut. Dad remained outside, surveying the campground below the hill. He felt the mighty gusts of wind pelting his skin with sand and dirt and saw a tsunami of dust engulfing the settlers below. A flash of lightning followed by the loud crack of thunder ushered in a torrential downpour. Dad ran inside where Mom sat holding Van and me in one corner, and the two sets of brothers retreated to their respective sections of the hut. The rain pounded the leaf roof, sounding like liquid pellets beating over our heads. The relentless wind peeled layers of palm fronds off the roof and allowed the rain to pour through. Everyone shuffled further inside the hut to avoid the gush of water pouring in. No matter where we sat, the wind managed to splash us with rain.

We huddled with the brothers, drenched from head to toe, shivering and praying for the rain to be over. My brother and I sat shaking. Dad noticed the tips of our fingers pruning and turning a shade of gray. He grabbed our hands and warmed them inside his while blowing warm air on our small fingers.

New refugees continued to spill into our camp without direction or support. International relief organizations tried to monitor the conditions, but the number and needs of the refugees overwhelmed the external organizations. Adults living in our camp understood the issues firsthand. They saw garbage discarded near living quarters, human waste buried indiscriminately, and petty theft committed among neighbors.

The day after the rain, Dad didn't want to waste the bucket of well water that Mom fetched that morning while he repaired the hut's roof with the brothers. He had no choice but to wash the feces off his feet. He walked into the brown pasty puddle, left by one of the neighbors, while he scavenged the area around our hut for palm leaves. "I always seem to step into it," Dad joked with Mom. They both tried to make light of the miserable conditions but knew the camp needed rules and order.

"Our neighbors don't seem to care about sanitation," Mom said. "There's a meeting down at the camp this evening. They're planning to elect a counsel and assign duties to improve camp life. You should go."

Before the sun set, Dad made his way along a trail that led him down the hill. He was by himself, surrounded only by the sounds of chirping birds. He passed a tree in bloom with flowers that had white and yellow petals. He caught a hint of jasmine as he passed the tree. Dad had seen the frangipani tree grown in the beach towns of Vietnam but, back then, he didn't care for flowers or appreciate their fragrance. He picked up a delicate flower from the ground and tucked it gently into his shirt pocket. He liked to surprise me and Mom with tiny perfumed flowers to chase away the scent of misery.

The trail's tranquil solitude ended when he arrived at the camp center. Before him stood ramshackle shelters squeezed in side by side. He heard young and old people coughing and hacking up phlegm, which they spat anywhere and everywhere near their dwellings. The tight living conditions caused tempers to flare. Dad often heard colorful quarrels from the adults while children and babies cried. Despite the unpleasantness, he liked the feeling of community and embraced the bustling energy of his fellow countrymen when he went to the heart of camp. At the same time, he couldn't wait to head back up the hill.

Dad walked into the camp church where a group gathered for the meeting. He recognized a few people from his hometown who had been civil and government leaders before the collapse of South Vietnam. He gave them a respectful nod and found a seat in the back of the room. He sat up straight, listening with interest, unlike the forced mass assemblies he'd known in the communist internment camp. He even stayed awake this time. He heard names nominated to head committees to address issues such as camp sanitation, English classes, and camp security.

Then he heard: "How about Brother Le to head up camp security?" A few people nodded. They knew of Dad's military background. The proposal caught him by surprise. He hesitated for a few seconds but accepted the volunteer position.

In the early morning, before everyone woke, Dad walked down the hill to meet his volunteer security team to start their day of patrol. A group of twenty young men, mostly former South Vietnamese soldiers and teenagers looking for a thrill with purpose, waited for him at the foot of the hill. They carried no sticks, knives, or weapons, as promised to the committee; the punishments they dispensed came in the form of stern warnings. The people in the camp, nonetheless, acknowledged them respectfully. They nodded and smiled when the group walked by. An elderly grandmother stopped Dad, took both of his hands, and said, "We have been victimized first by the communists and now by the Thai police. We have already experienced enough suffering."

Life in the refugee camp had a predictable pattern of monotony. In the morning, Dad left to patrol the camp. At home, weakened by hunger, Mom, Van, and I gathered dry firewood. The brothers who shared our shelter fetched drinking water from a well inside the camp. Mom dug a small pit in the ground to start a fire to later cook our one meal of rice in the late afternoon. She washed clothes without soap. When not working, she patiently waited for the days to pass.

Once a week, she went down the hill with Van and me to stand in line to collect a small bag of rice and two small mullet fish; no fresh fruit or vegetables came with the handout. Each time Mom waited in line holding a cloth sack and our tiny hands, one on each side, she worried about how she could stretch the scanty amount of food over the week for our family.

During one wait in the food line, Mom tilted her body to the side to look at the mass of people in front of her. She saw young and old men and women, their gaunt sun-weathered bodies and solemn faces showing acceptance of poverty and hunger—but only for the time being. Hope still fed their stomachs, as it had on the boat. They chattered the same talk about how different life would be in America, Europe, Canada, or Australia. Their faces perked up when hearing news of refugees settling in the western countries.

Mom noticed that the line moved slower that day than most. When her turn came, she opened her cloth sack for the worker to throw in the rice and two fish the size of her slender forearm. Before she turned away, the worker gave us each a biscuit cookie and cups of warm powdered milk. This was the reason for the extra wait, as everyone in line received the welcome treat.

Mom took a sip of the warm, creamy drink and felt the tension and worry that had been hammering at her melt away. She'd drunk plenty of powdered milk and finer beverages in her life, but nothing tasted sweeter than in that moment. She took her cookie and showed Van and me how to dunk it in our cups to make it softer. My brother and I gobbled up our cookie before it touched the milk.

On his walk home one evening, after spending much of the day breaking up squabbles and a gambling ring, it occurred to Dad that his new role was a punishment for being a menace in his youth. He reasoned that if it weren't for camp rules and his new title, he wouldn't mind sitting down with some of the guys he'd just reprimand and play a few hands of cards with them. He also remembered it was my birthday. I turned five, and he didn't have anything to give me.

Before hiking up the hill, Dad made a turn for the beach. He knew I liked to go to there, sometimes by myself, to watch froth and bubbles form when the waves crashed against the rocks. He found me sitting by myself on a large black boulder, with my thin arms wrapped around my legs, looking—almost mesmerized—into the water as the fluffy white suds formed and evaporated. He looked around and saw no one; only the seagulls circling above in a grayish blue evening sky. Dad wondered why I would be drawn to this lonely but serene beach. He had warned me about going near the water by myself. And like the camp violators to whom he issued warnings, I politely nodded but resumed my activities. He didn't know that when I had a group of friends with me, we would jump from one slippery boulder to the next. The cracks in between were wide and deep—large enough to encase a small child.

"Happy birthday, daughter," he said and sat down beside me. "This time next year, we'll be in our new home, and I'll get you a real gift. Until then . . ." He pulled out a single plum-sized plumeria flower from his pocket and tucked it in my hair.

"Where is our new home?" I asked. It was a question he had asked himself ever since we arrived at the refugee camp. Dad didn't know how long we would be there, or which western country would accept us for resettlement. He just hoped his promise held true.

The cool evening breeze blew on our skin, and he saw the tiny goose bumps pop up on my lanky arms. The briny, fishy smell of the ocean made him think of supper, but he knew there would only be plain white rice waiting for us.

"Let's head back," he finally said. He lifted me up and swung me onto his shoulder; my skinny legs dangled on his chest. I held on to both of his ears as we made our way up the hill.

EACH MONTH, A DELEGATION from different western countries like the United States, Australia,

Canada, France, Germany, and the United Kingdom visited the camp and interviewed refugees to determine eligibility for permanent resettlement into their country. The United States took in the most refugees, but there was a process with paperwork and interviews that we had to undergo. Many people wanted acceptance into the United States. At the time, the US gave priority to refugees who could prove political persecution due to their past affiliation with the South Vietnamese military or government. Word circulated among the adults that they had to be careful with their interview answers.

"Make sure you both have your facts correct during the interview, or you'll have to fix this hut for a longer stay," Toan counseled my parents the night before they went for the interview.

The American refugee caseworker reviewed Dad's file and asked, "Did you encounter any persecution after the Vietnam War from your affiliation with the South Vietnamese military or government?"

"Yes," Dad answered and thought how simple his reply sounded for such a tangled tragedy.

The interviewer went on to ask how many years he spent in the military and in the internment camp, the name of his unit, and his rank. Mom confirmed Dad's response by giving the simple, but truthful, answer.

One week after the interview, Dad stopped by the beach on his way home to check on me. He found me in the same spot, sitting on the boulder enchanted by the foam and froth created by the crashing waves.

"I have your answer. Our new home is in America." Dad smiled at me. I smiled back, showing a missing front tooth.

Toan and his brother, Chuong, interviewed during the same period. Their entry to the US, however, was denied because the brothers gave different answers during the interview. When the interviewer asked Toan how many homes their family owned in Vietnam, he stated "one." When the question was repeated to the younger brother, Chuong, who was not paying attention, he declared that the family had two homes. Technically their family did have two homes: the main house and a shed. A huge spat erupted in the hut between the two brothers that night. They remained in the refugee camp for an additional three years before Australia accepted them for resettlement. Sang and Diep went to Canada soon after we left.

When our time to leave came, Dad grabbed a worn leather suitcase that contained everything that we owned: one set of clothes for each person and an envelope of old photos. Mom took my hand along with Van's and followed Dad down the hill for the last time.

The brothers walked with us. Toan's eyes brimmed with tears, but he did not want anyone to see him cry. Dad shook the brothers' hands and bowed his head; we had been a family for twelve months.

From the bus window, Dad waved farewell to the brothers and wondered if he would ever see them again. Our family waved until the brothers and the camp became tiny specks in the background. Dad turned away and looked forward. The bus sped from the refugee camp to Bangkok.

The bustle of city life in Bangkok reminded Dad of Saigon, but we did not have the freedom to explore. We arrived at another government warehouse where three hundred other refugees from various camps in Thailand were housed. We claimed a small area in the open space to settle until we could leave Bangkok.

Dad took out a blanket and laid it on the concrete floor. We rested on the blanket and waited. We watched other refugees in the warehouse move about, passing the time—mothers consoling their crying babies, a grandmother holding a handkerchief over her mouth while coughing, and children chasing each other. All around, the strong menthol smell of eucalyptus oil soothed the homesick.

Only the aroma of curried chicken that was brought out for dinner could chase away the pervasive menthol scent that is believed to be a cure-all by most Vietnamese mothers. The smell of onion, cumin, and garlic made Dad's mouth water. He rushed our family to get in line. Each person grabbed a small plastic plate from the pile. The Thai workers scooped a ladle of rice and chicken curry onto each plate.

Dad was famished. "Can I have a little more?" he asked.

He received a flat, expressionless, "No."

We returned to our little spot to eat. The chicken and coconut curry disappeared from Dad's plate before the rest of us finished eating. I scooped several spoonsful of my food onto his plate.

"It's too spicy for me," I told him.

Everyone living in the warehouse waited in limbo, some longer than others. We had to pass the medical clearance for communicable diseases such as tuberculosis before we could leave. Anyone identified with exposure to tuberculosis or who had the active disease had to stay in Bangkok to finish treatments. After one week, my family received the green light to leave. Late at night, when the warehouse went dark and its residents were asleep, Dad carried my sleeping older brother in one arm and the lone leather suitcase in the other hand. Mom held my hand and we followed Dad out of the warehouse.

On that November night in 1979, we boarded a DC-10 Transamerica plane to the US with a refueling stop in Okinawa. The flight attendant smiled and welcomed us on board. My brother and I were unaware of the significance of each stop on our voyage out of Vietnam. But for my parents, that first step entering the plane was like a giant leap into a new life. Dad sat back and closed his eyes. He did not have to worry about being shot at when the plane lifted off the runway. For the first time in several years, we received more food than we could eat.

Dad's attention turned to me when he caught me sniffing a box of Crayola crayons given out by the flight attendant. He watched with amusement as I studied the crayons with their homey, edible aroma, tempting me to taste them. But I didn't. It was the first time Van and I had ever seen a box of crayons or coloring books.

Peering outside the plane window at the layers of white clouds, Dad saw a boundless blue sea below and knew we must be somewhere over the Pacific Ocean. He had nothing to do but let his mind wander.

Dad agonized over the people swept up with him in the mayhem, whose whereabouts were lost. He wondered about his army brothers, Colonel Hai and General Di. Were they still alive?

So much had transpired over what seemed like a lifetime ago. Dad was only thirty-one. He remembered that during the war an elderly village man with a wispy white beard had predicted that he would no longer be in Vietnam after the age of thirty-one. He hadn't believed the prediction.

CHAPTER 18

America

AS THE DC-10 DESCENDED into San Francisco on the evening of November 28, 1979, Dad gazed out the window. Below, he saw the glow of car lights along the ribbons of highways. The first image of America that caught his eyes was not the Golden Gate Bridge; it was the freeways at night.

Dad loved to drive. He thought the endless winding trails of red car lights below glowed like the tail of a mythical dragon in the night. A sense of awe and intimidation swept over him. He leaned over and said to Mom, "I wonder if I can drive in America like I did in Vietnam?"

Late that night, we landed at a military air station in Oakland, California. Dad's heart raced as the plane touched down and slowed to a stop. He looked out the window like a kid on a new adventure, curious and wanting to take in as much as his eyes could see.

We huddled close to Dad when we got off the plane and walked onto the tarmac. A gust of frigid autumn wind pierced through our light clothes and sandals, alerting us that we were no longer in the tropics. We filed into a military warehouse along with other refugees from the same flight.

The American female relief worker asked in English for Dad's residency paperwork that had been initiated in Thailand. He had not studied English in school, and he knew only a few words from the introductory classes in the refugee camp. She repeated the question, slower and louder. Dad pulled out the documents and hoped it was what she wanted. A staff member from the American Fund for Czechoslovak Refugees (AFCR) came over and assisted.

The AFCR helped those from Czechoslovakia, as well as Hungarians, Poles, Romanians, and Bulgarians, who escaped communist expansion in Eastern Europe during the Cold War. The organization assisted in resettling displaced refugees in Europe and America. In 1979, the AFCR offered its humanitarian services to refugees from Southeast Asia by matching American sponsors with refugees. They worked in conjunction with the International Refugee Organization (IRO) and the UNHCR.

After completing the paperwork, we joined the other refugees and boarded a bus that took us to a nearby motel. Feeling overwhelmed, Dad worried from his encounter in the warehouse how he would navigate through his first months of life in America without knowledge of the English language. At the same time, he felt tired and just wanted to find a place to sleep.

The motel room had two queen-size beds with red satin covers, sitting on orange shag carpet in the style of the '70s. But to us, it was a luxurious haven. We would sleep on a bed instead of a cement or bamboo floor. Although the room had a stale odor of cigarette smoke, it was preferable to the stench of sweat and grime from a swarm of desperate people deprived of human comfort and dignity. The bathroom's running water meant no hauling well water for bucket baths. An old box television with three channels sat on top of a dresser. Van and I spent part of the night turning the TV's knobs back and forth and adjusting the volume dial as though it were a new toy. Dad was tired from the long plane ride and apprehensive about his unfamiliarity with America. However, for the first time in a long while, he felt safe.

The next morning, we ate breakfast inside a school bus parked outside the motel that had been converted to a diner. Our stomachs weren't used to breakfast but welcomed it. For the past year, our first and only meal for the day had not started until late afternoon. Dad ate the eggs and ham from own his plate and finished the leftover food off of mine. Van and I contently chewed on our red apple and sipped sweet iced tea, a staple that came with every meal on the school bus. Along with the smell of a fresh box of crayons, the taste of a crisp red apple washed down with iced tea became one of my first sense memories of America.

After a month of our living in the motel, the AFCR moved us into an old two-story Victorian house on Mission Street near downtown San Francisco with three other refugee families. Each family occupied a bedroom and shared the kitchen. The living room was a dark empty space without furniture. We slept on mattresses, squeezed next to one another on the floor. Our housemates came from Cambodia and Laos. Other than offering polite smiles when passing in the hall, the other families kept to themselves. Dad tried to start conversations with them, but none knew the other's language or English.

The AFCR began the search for a sponsor family for us. They found a retired Army colonel in Utah who had served in Vietnam and who was eager to help us. The colonel phoned Dad and said, "*Chao, Anh.*"

Dad, startled by the pleasant greeting, replied, "Hello, Brother." The colonel was not Vietnamese but spoke the language with a smooth South Vietnamese accent.

Over the next hour, the colonel shared his favorite memories of life in Saigon—the fishy whiff of *nuoc mam* in every restaurant and the garlicky aroma of street food floating along the tight alleyways. Talk of food always made Dad happy. After the phone call, he felt good about the colonel from Utah, who was a Mormon. He and Mom discussed moving to Utah. He knew nothing about Utah or Mormonism until he learned from his cousin, Vinh, who had settled in Nebraska a few years earlier, that Mormons abstained from alcohol and tobacco.

Dad lit a cigarette from the pack in his shirt pocket and pondered as he exhaled a stream of smoke whether he would be able to adapt to this culture even though the wholesome atmosphere sounded good for our family. As they had with past decisions, his vices won, and he politely declined the kind offer.

On their second attempt, the AFCR matched us with a San Francisco family, the Oritas. We moved into John and Mary Orita's spacious home with a backyard swimming pool. The Oritas were in their fifties with two pre-teen daughters. Mr. Orita ran a gas station, and his wife worked from home as an accountant. They were a blend of no-nonsense strictness and compassion. They heard about our family through their church and learned from the evening news about the displaced Vietnamese refugees. Like most Americans, they had followed the Vietnam War on the evening news. When the opportunity was presented for them to help, they volunteered.

Dad thought the Oritas kept a tidy home even though he didn't get to see the entire house. Mary guided us directly to our bedrooms. She opened the door to a room with a bunk bed, which she had prepared for Van and me. She pointed my parents to the adjacent room. Mary handed us a stack of towels and went over the house rules, which included no eating in the bedrooms. When she left, Van and I made a beeline for our parents' room. We were used to a confined living space and did not want to be separated from our parents in another strange environment. Our family of four stayed together in one bedroom and, out of politeness, did not venture to other parts of the house.

In the morning, John Orita left for work and Mary went into the study to start tapping on her adding machine. The loud clicking and sputtering noise signaled to us that we had to keep quiet while she worked. Van and I spent most of the day inside the bedroom watching television while Dad and Mom took an English class. While our parents studied English in the classroom, we learned English from television shows like *The Dukes of Hazzard* and hummed along to the theme song of *Gilligan's Island*.

Mealtime followed a set schedule, with planned menus. The Oritas' weight-loss diet excluded white rice, which was a staple for our family. Instead, they ate small portions of boiled vegetables and pieces of lean chicken. My family, already stick-thin from years of deprivation, ate the same meal. Dad grumbled after supper one night, "The guy on the boat who joked about all the food we would eat in America never heard about a diet."

After three weeks with the Oritas and four months in America, we were on the move again. While my parents felt grateful to the Oritas, they wanted to work and have their own home. Dad's cousin, Vinh, urged him to come to Nebraska, where he promised to help my parents find work. With help from the AFCR, Dad purchased four Greyhound bus tickets to Hastings, Nebraska. We packed all our possessions into the same leather suitcase we brought from Vietnam. Our only new clothing was winter coats, given to us by the ACFR, which we still needed, going to Nebraska in March 1980. With three hundred dollars left in Dad's pocket, one suitcase of clothes, and a bag of cookies from Mrs. Orita, we boarded the bus for Nebraska.

Before he got on the bus, Dad shook John Orita's hand and thanked him. Mr. Orita looked a little hurt and said, "You guys just got here. I can help you find a job." Dad wanted to explain to John Orita but did not have the English to tell him that we had taken so many risks already in search of freedom and a home; we had to keep going.

The bus traveled through northern California to Nevada, Utah, Wyoming, and then finally Nebraska. We travelled halfway across the country, from the West Coast to the Midwest, and saw the ingenuity and beauty of America. The highway route out of California paralleled the first transcontinental railroad that linked the East Coast to the West, built mostly by Chinese immigrants.

We saw the silver hills and tanned grass that covered the mountains of Nevada, Utah, and Wyoming. We passed through the snowcapped mountains of the Sierra Nevada, crossed the Rocky Mountains, then to the plains and corn-fields of the Midwest. We didn't realize that during the jour-ney from California to the heartland we shared a path that thousands of Americans took during the westward migra-tion in the 1800s. We did not know while passing through Wyoming that, over a hundred years before, American set-tlers on the Oregon, Mormon, and California trail etched their names on a large granite rock, not far from our bus route. The 130-foot-high edifice became a historic land-mark known as Independence Rock. Even though we were going in the opposite direction from the westward settlers, we all searched for the same thing: a better life.

Along the way, there were stops in small towns and big cities. With little knowledge of the English language, my parents kept to themselves on the bus. My brother and I were not shy and sang songs that we learned in English, such as "Old MacDonald," to the delight of a few bus passengers. They clapped and encouraged us to keep singing. After each encore, we sang louder, with more confidence, until Dad had to silence us for the other passengers trying to sleep.

During a stop in Nevada, Mom got out to look for sodas to buy for our thirsty family. She saw a shop with the word she recognized, Coca-Cola. The strong scent of alcohol hit her nostrils when she walked in.

The man behind the counter asked, "What can I get for you, honey?"

She timidly replied, "Please, you give me four cups of Coca-Cola."

The bartender laughed and said, "You talk like a baby!"

Trying to speak English *did* make her feel like a child learning to speak for the first time. He asked her some questions, but he spoke too fast for her to follow. The bartender muttered a few words under his breath and gave her the drinks. Not sure of what he said, she felt angered by the treatment and took the sodas back to the bus.

We waited eagerly for the drinks. Mom, Van, and I took one sip and grimaced at the burning concoction mixed with sugared Coca-Cola. We couldn't finish the drinks. Dad, however, had a contented smile on his face while he gulped down his own beverage and finished the other three cups spiked with alcohol.

The snow came down hard and the roads became slick with ice when we crossed Wyoming. The bus driver had to pull over to put snow chains on the bus tires. While the bus sat there, Dad handed chicken sandwiches to us. He had purchased the food earlier at a stop, thanks to the help of a bus passenger. He was still unfamiliar with using the American dollar.

"A passenger showed me how to use what's called a vending machine. I put coins in, chose the food I want, and out pops my selection—amazing!" Dad marveled.

He then remembered another purchase. He pulled out a bagful of individually wrapped pieces of milk chocolate. He hadn't meant to get a whole bagful. When the cashier asked him how much candy he wanted, Dad handed her a five-dollar bill—not knowing how much it could buy in 1980. Van and I didn't mind; the candy gave us energy to sing with more gusto on the bus.

In the late evening of the second day, the bus approached the outskirts of Hastings, Nebraska. The farmland, with rows of tilled soil, waited for the spring corn crop. Following wide-open farmlands and endless sky, the bus rolled toward the small town. Old-fashioned buildings lined the streets alongside wood-framed homes with trim yards.

Dad saw a sign that said, "Welcome to Hastings, Nebraska—The Town Where Kool-Aid Was Invented." He had never heard of Kool-Aid, but it would soon become a favorite drink for my brother and me. The bus stopped at a grocery store in the quaint downtown where shops of blue, white, and pink stood wall to wall next to each other like in a picture postcard illustrating the charms of small-town America.

Peering out the bus window, Dad recognized his cousin, Vinh, waving. Vinh had shaggy shoulder-length hair and a mustache, a popular look of the time. He wore a dark tan leather jacket with bell-bottom trousers. Dad hadn't seen his cousin in over a decade but guessed it must be him since he was the only Asian man in the crowd. Vinh didn't have a problem recognizing us either; we were the only Asian family on the bus. Dad started to feel a little homesick but reminded himself that the home he knew was no more. He was in Hastings now, the home of Kool-Aid.

CHAPTER 19

Fortitude

DAD OPENED THE DOOR and led us inside our first home in America. The upstairs, two-bedroom apartment overlooked North Kansas Avenue, across the street from the town's hospital. The landlady, a widow, lived downstairs. She charged us one hundred fifty dollars a month in rent. After Dad paid an advance on the first month's rent, he had only one hundred dollars left in his pocket, which meant furnishings and home goods had to wait.

Vinh gave us blankets, which we spread on the floor for beds. Dad's cousin, a bachelor in his thirties, had come to Hastings five years earlier. How he found Hastings was a mystery to Dad. But Vinh, different from most unattached men of his age, did not prefer big-city excitement. Vinh appreciated the quiet streets, the serene farms, and the Midwestern friendliness of Hastings.

Bedding and furniture were not urgencies for Dad. He wanted food. We were all hungry. Not eating much on the bus and dieting with the Oritas left us famished.

Vinh drove us to the grocery store three miles from our apartment. Dad's eyes lit up when he entered the supermarket. The inside felt just as cold as the chilly spring night. The door opened to the produce section, and Dad could smell the sugary scent of fruit mixed with the floral tang of disinfectant, a contrast to the natural fragrance of sun-ripened fruit sold in the open street markets back in Vietnam. He did not expect the grocery store to have the tropical fruit that he craved—like durian, which gave off an incredibly strong odor of musky, ripe cheese. No air conditioning or deodorizer in the world could mask that distinct pungency.

Our total at check-out came to twenty dollars. Dad looked at his basket and wondered if he should put something back, but after hesitating, he handed the money to the cashier, knowing that his funds would run out soon.

Vinh drove us home. On the way back, Dad memorized the route. He anticipated walking back to the market; he couldn't keep asking Vinh for help. What he didn't know at the time was that Vinh had already put the word out that a young Vietnamese family, new to America, had arrived in town.

Within a week of settling into our new home, we got a knock at the door. In front of Dad stood two men in their forties. They extended their hands and introduced themselves.

"I'm Neil Grothen," said the man with sandy blond hair and a farmer's tan.

"And I'm Larry Schutte," said the other man. "We heard about your family from our church and wanted to stop by to offer our help."

Dad was reluctant to invite them inside. Nonetheless, from where they were standing, Neil and Larry could see the bare apartment. Dad wasn't sure how to respond to them. He just wanted a job to provide for his family. Not knowing what to expect, Dad accepted their overture.

On a snowy day in Hastings, Nebraska, the Grothens introduce my family to the joy of sledding. Van makes his way up the hill to slide down on his saucer again while the Grothen children and I trail behind. (Courtesy of Tran B. Quan)

The next morning, the two men returned with their families—Neil and his wife, Joyce, with their two children, Grant and Gayla, and Larry with his wife, Velda, and their two sons. They carried bags of collected clothes, pots, pans, utensils, and toys. They stacked everything in the apartment. Then they handed Dad an envelope that contained two hundred dollars. They asked Dad to accept the church collection. Larry's sons had broken their piggy banks and donated sixty dollars of their own savings. Mom stood next to Dad, her eyes filled with tears. She bowed her head to show her gratitude. Dad wished he knew the right English words to express his gratefulness. All he could say was, "Thank you."

More church members stopped by after that first visit. They brought more donated goods. Even strangers stopped their cars to offer Dad a ride home when they saw him

Me, Dad, and John Deere in Nebraska, 1980. (Courtesy of Tran B. Quan)

walking from the grocery store with Van carrying bags of groceries.

EVEN THOUGH THE CALENDAR indicated spring, it still snowed in Hastings. The white flakes clung to bare tree branches, roofs, and the lawns of homes and fertile farm acres. On some days, the winter clouds blocked the sun, and Hastings was engulfed in a white fog of snow. When the sun came out again, it was not enough to melt the accumulated ivory powder. Hastings became a frosted wonderland. On snowy nights, my brother and I sat by the window watching the fluffy white flakes fall, illuminated by the streetlights. We had seen snow in San Francisco and on the bus ride to Nebraska but had never played in it—until the Grothens took us sledding.

The Grothens brought us to one of the hills in town. They had packed metal saucer sleds and an old toboggan. Grant and Gayla took the first slide down the hill to demonstrate. Van and I spun down the hill together on the saucer, screaming and laughing. My parents followed in the toboggan.

Snow got inside our shoes and soaked our socks, but that did not stop us from repeated runs down the hill. When sprinkles of white flakes dropped from the clouds, Van and I stuck out our tongues to taste the snow, something we had seen the other kids do. Dad believed we were like sponges soaking up the new customs much faster than he and Mom could. He was happy to see us assimilating to our new culture. At the same time, he worried that he and Mom would not have the time to spend with us to ensure we did not forget our Vietnamese heritage and language.

Even during war and imprisonment, Dad never lost his sense of fun. He was touched that Neil and Joyce not only provided our family with the practical necessities but also brought back an enjoyable side to life.

The snow came down harder, and the frigid air froze his nose hair, but Dad felt warm watching me and my brother giggling and throwing snowballs at each other and at the Grothens. The goodness he found in Hastings cooled the memories of the flames and heat of war.

On the weekends, the Grothens drove our family to their farm for cookouts. Dad asked Neil to show him his tractors. Neil opened the barn door where his massive green John Deere tractors rested during the winter. The small tractor that Dad had used for a short time in Vietnam could not compare.

"Do you want to give it a try?" Neil offered. With Neil sitting beside him, Dad took the tractor out of the barn and drove it to the nearby field. Neil showed him how to operate the tractor attachments as they chugged along. Dad thought he wouldn't mind being a farmer with this equipment.

While riding in the tractor, the urge to find work gnawed at Dad again. He also wanted his own car. Without hesitation, he got a driver's license during the first month in Hastings but had no money for a vehicle. Dad checked with Vinh every few days on the prospect of work but had no luck, for the American economy was slowing down in 1980.

The answer to Dad's prayers for work came one day at church when Mr. Chuck came up to Dad and introduced himself. The Grothens invited our family to church even though my parents were Buddhists and did not have plans to convert. Nonetheless, they attended services to show their gratitude to the community that welcomed us.

Mr. Chuck, a native New Yorker in his fifties, was the superintendent of T-L Irrigation Company. Underneath his burly, gruff exterior, he had a soft spot for the disadvantaged. He had heard about Dad and decided to find a job somewhere in the company for him, even though business had slowed and hiring was halted.

"Come to the company on Monday morning. I have a job for you," Mr. Chuck offered.

Dad was not a religious man. As a Buddhist, he rarely attended temple services. But after Mr. Chuck's offer, he closed his eyes and silently said a prayer of gratitude inside the church.

DAD GOT UP BEFORE dawn, filled his thermos with hot coffee, and placed a container of leftover food into his lunch bag. He waited outside the apartment house for Vinh to come and pick him up. Vinh dropped him off at T-L before heading to his own job. Dad stood outside the building, waiting in the predawn darkness before work started. When Mr. Chuck arrived, he saw Dad standing by himself warming his hands inside his pockets from the morning chill. He opened the door and showed Dad inside.

"You're the first one here. How long have you been waiting?" Mr. Chuck asked.

"One hour. My cousin give me ride," Dad answered.

Mr. Chuck started Dad off with boxing farm irrigation parts. Dad worked nonstop until he completed his assignment, making sure that each part laid securely inside the box. Feeling obliged for the work, he wanted to do a good job. Dad also did not want to be the target of Mr. Chuck's wrath. Every few hours, he heard Mr. Chuck yell at the workers in a booming voice from the second-floor office. Mr. Chuck had a clear view of the activities below. He could see who slacked off.

When Dad's shift ended and all the employees left, he sat waiting for his ride home. Mr. Chuck noticed and told Dad, "Grab a broom and start sweeping." He wanted to give Dad overtime work while he waited. Mr. Chuck continued, "I'll pick you up for work tomorrow morning."

Mr. Chuck was loud, blunt, and wore a constant scowl on his face, but Dad knew he had a heart of gold. He gave Dad three raises in six months. Even though each wage increase was only twenty-five cents an hour, it helped. Mom also found work, cleaning a nearby machine shop. Combined, the wages helped them scratch out a modest, but stable, income.

After four months of work, Dad saved enough money for a car. Dad knew he had found his car when he saw the light blue 1975 Ford station wagon in the used car lot. It was like meeting a new friend that he knew would be loyal and true. They would be together for the long haul, through smooth rides and rough. He paid eight hundred dollars for the station wagon and beamed with pride driving it out of the lot. This was a milestone for Dad.

Spring matured to summer, and the farm fields shot up rows of tall green stalks of corn that swayed like green waves in an ocean when a gust of wind blew through. The school year ended; I had spent most of it sitting in a corner as punishment for not paying attention to the teachers. Van and I were both enrolled in kindergarten, but while Van was promoted to the first grade, I flunked. My teacher met with Dad after school and explained that I lacked the maturity to progress. When the meeting ended, Dad found me sitting outside on the school bench by myself waiting for him. I watched the flicker of sunlight through a tree fall on my fingers. I didn't say anything when he sat down next to me. I kept my head bent. I guessed that whatever the teacher told him hadn't been good. I knew my parents worked long hours and didn't have the time to come to my school unless it was bad. After a long stretch of silence, Dad wrapped one arm around my small frame and said, "I got in trouble a lot in school."

FALL CAME, AND I returned to kindergarten. Farmers gathered their harvest. The leaves changed from a vibrant summer green to the rich orange and red shades of autumn. The biggest change, however, was that the country sank into the recession of the early 1980s. Dad saw workers, one by one, get laid off that fall and wondered when he would be next.

He asked Mr. Chuck half timidly and half seriously, "When will I go?"

Mr. Chuck answered, "When the company closes." Dad felt warmed, hearing this reassurance, but he knew the reality would soon come. Mom received her pink slip, and our family now relied solely on Dad's small paycheck. With the three pay raises that Mr. Chuck had given him, Dad's salary was up to five dollars an hour.

The blue Nebraska summer skies turned gray and overcast when fall approached. The mood at the irrigation company became somber like the fall sky as more workers were laid off. Dad learned that the Vu family, a Vietnamese couple in Hastings that my parents befriended, decided to leave town after both husband and wife lost their jobs. Mr. and Mrs. Vu planned to head east to Maryland, where they knew friends who could help them find work. They persuaded my parents to join them.

Another change coming to our family would be the addition of a new baby. My parents were expecting their third child. Dad had more reasons to worry about money.

DAD SAT IN THE blue station wagon for a few minutes before heading into work. He tried to find the best words he knew in English to tell Mr. Chuck that he was leaving. He wanted Mr. Chuck to know how grateful he felt. He found Mr. Chuck sitting in his office reviewing a stack of papers.

"What can I do for you, Le?" he asked.

Before Dad could even finish stringing his words together, Mr. Chuck stopped him and tried to convince Dad to stay.

Dad did not know how to respond. Mr. Chuck relented. Without saying another word, Mr. Chuck took a sheet of paper and started writing. Dad stood watching and waiting. He did not have a clue what Mr. Chuck was doing. When done, Mr. Chuck looked over the letter of recommendation he had written, then signed his name next to his contact information.

"Give this to your next employer, Le. I will vouch that you are a good man." Mr. Chuck handed Dad the letter.

"You are also a good man, Mr. Chuck," Dad said to his boss.

Telling Mr. Chuck goodbye was hard, but Dad felt worse breaking the news to friends like the Grothens and Schuttes. Neil told him that he and Joyce planned to visit once we got settled.

Joyce, only a few years older than Dad, gave him some parting advice he never forgot. "Be cautious. You will find that not everyone will be as welcoming as the people of Hastings." Dad nodded. Hastings, for our family, had been like being wrapped in a warm, soft blanket after being out in the cold rain.

WE FINISHED LOADING THE station wagon by nightfall. We packed the donated clothes, dishes, pots, pans, blankets, and pillows and then squeezed it all into and on top of the station wagon. When we finished, the tires sagged even before we left the driveway. Dad pulled out a map to trace the route across five states to Maryland.

Dad drove the bulging station wagon along the interstate, following the Vu family across the plains. He found a relaxing sense of freedom on the long stretches of highway. While everyone slept, Dad saw more of America. He didn't mind that other cars flew past him as he kept a steady pace toward Maryland.

When the Vus' car lagged behind, he pulled to the side of the interstate to wait. A police officer noticed our family of four squeezed into the overloaded station wagon, looking like the Beverly Hillbillies. The officer turned on his siren. Dad thought he was about to get his first traffic ticket. To his relief, the policeman asked if we needed help.

Dad drove three days and two nights straight and arrived at a chicken processing plant in Salisbury, Maryland. Fresh from the road, without a home or an unpacked vehicle, my parents walked into the factory. Immediately, a noxious odor of poultry guts, blood, and chicken poop hit them. The stink triggered Mom's morning sickness. She wanted to cover her nose with her hands, but she didn't want to appear rude, especially since she needed this job. Instead, she placed her hand over her belly, which was not showing signs of the expected baby yet. Only Dad knew that she was pregnant. Without saying a word, he squeezed her hand.

Mr. Vu's friend introduced them to the factory's hiring manager. The chicken factory needed hard workers. The manager must have sensed that my parents would do back-breaking work and not complain much. He hired them on the spot. They started two days later.

The freshly gutted chicken, plucked and slaughtered minutes before at a different station on the assembly line, hung upside down by its claws and came on a hanger to Dad. He had to pull the chicken off the hanger hook and throw it into a cart where it later moved to Mom's section for washing and packaging. One by one, he pulled dead chickens off the moving carousel that circled by him. Once he got into the groove, he pulled at least forty chickens off the hanger carousel every minute. His arms ached but, as the hiring manager expected, he didn't complain.

Dad found a furnished trailer for two hundred dollars a month. The clean and simple trailer sat in a quiet corner next to a few homes in a wooded area. The neighbors kept to themselves, avoiding us. They didn't come by to introduce themselves like the people of Hastings. They watched from behind half-drawn window curtains.

Even with both salaries, my parents could barely afford rent for the trailer. They each made four dollars an hour. On some weeks they had less than ten dollars in their pockets before the next paycheck. But they were happy. We had all the chicken we could eat at a discounted price. Sometimes my parents took their last ten dollars and treated us to a drive-in movie.

In Maryland, we discovered crabbing. Blue crabs were bountiful along the piers. Workers at the plant taught my parents to use chicken as bait.

On a free weekend, without money for other forms of entertainment, my parents took a bag of chicken parts to the pier and threw a chicken thigh tied to string into the water. They couldn't spare money for a net, so Dad found a mesh strainer with a handle in the trailer's kitchen to substitute. Within seconds of throwing the bait into the water, three to four crabs grabbed on to the chicken part. Mom shrieked with excitement, pointing at the catch. Dad reached into the water with the strainer and scooped up the hungry crabs. A few fell out of the small strainer and splashed back into the water. On their first attempt at crabbing, my parents managed to fill a paper bag full of blue crabs.

We didn't need money to be happy, but with a new baby coming and more expenses, Dad decided to find a more affordable place to live. He discovered that the factory had living quarters reserved at a cut rate for workers. The drab, concrete one-story building comprised an arrangement similar to that of a roadside motel. The low price matched the poor conditions. Dad paid fifty dollars a month for a filthy one-room studio that had stained cement floors and walls. The room had just enough space for two beds lined against the walls. A stove sat in a corner. We shared a communal bathroom with the other tenants.

The new baby girl arrived and came home in November 1980. My parents named her Thanh. The baby had chubby pink cheeks and a healthy appetite. Mom believed that all the blue crabs she ate made the baby robust.

Soon, Dad felt we had to move again. The poor living conditions pushed him to find a better place despite his lack of funds. Our stability and comfort seemed dependent on money, which was always in short supply.

Dad found a small summer lake house for rent. It was located in a park where clusters of similar rental cottages stood, most vacated as fall and winter arrived. The property manager gave Dad a discount, since no one rented during the winter. Plus, he saw in us children potential playmates for his son, Eric, who didn't have any friends during the cold months.

The lakeside property turned empty and silent in winter like the stillness after a party. The lake that during the summer teemed with boats and canoes froze over the winter. The sound of laughter from the only school-aged children on the property broke the silence. Eric joined Van and me zigzagging through the trees, stirring up the dried, crinkled maple leaves from the ground during games of tag.

School remained a struggle for me even though my brother and I had a good command of English by then. I found myself in the corner again for being loud or fighting with the boys on the playground. When I got frustrated with the teachers or mad at my classmates, I screamed at them in Vietnamese. The other kids didn't dare tease me; they just ignored me.

When report cards were handed out, I came home empty-handed. Van showed my parents his good marks, but when they asked for my report card I looked down and said quietly, "The teacher didn't give me one."

I didn't tell them that while the kids in my class were learning reading, writing, and arithmetic, I was sent to art, lunch, and recess throughout the day. My teachers didn't think I was educable and thus improvised a special curriculum for me. At first, I didn't mind. But soon I noticed the different treatment. So did the other kids, who complained that they also wanted double recess and lunch. Consequently, I fell even further behind in school.

Dad watched me study Van's report card with the checks and check-plus marks next to sentences I couldn't read. I knew my ABC's and could count to twenty, having watched *Sesame Street*, but I wanted to know how to put the letters together to reveal the puzzle that I felt everyone knew, except me.

Dad felt bad for me. I reminded him of himself in school. He wished he could help me, but his immediate concerns were to feed and shelter our family. He patted my shoulder and said, "I believe in you."

CHAPTER 20

Texas

WHEN THE WINTER SNOW melted and spring bloomed in Maryland, Dad received a letter from a friend in Texas who persuaded him to move for the warm weather, the new job possibilities, and the large Vietnamese community in Houston. He yearned for all three.

Dad gave the letter to Mom and went outside to inspect his faithful station wagon. He kicked the worn tires and glided his hand over the smooth treads—all four tires needed to be changed. But he couldn't afford new tires. "Think you can make it to Texas?" he asked the old car. He often talked to it like it was part of the family.

Nomadic wandering still coursed in my parents' blood as they continued to search for a permanent home and community. This time, Texas beckoned us.

Before we left Maryland, Dad purchased two recapped tires to replace the worst ones and prayed that the other two would last all the way to Texas. He didn't tell Mom that if the tires blew along the way, we would be stranded without money for repair. With less than two hundred dollars in his pocket, Dad could only afford a bag of oranges for us to nibble on during the trip. His eyes stayed alert to every pothole and piece of debris on the road. He thanked the cool weather of late spring for not stressing the tires.

After 1,500 miles, we made it to Houston. Right away, we could see and feel a difference. The tall skyscrapers of downtown stood like concrete-and-glass mountains. The spring temperature in Houston was like that of a summer day up north. The notorious heat and humidity of the triple-digit summer had not yet made their debut.

Within a week of arriving in Houston, my parents found work as janitors, followed by a string of temporary jobs. They rented a two-bedroom apartment in the Spring Branch district of Houston, where the neighbors came from different ethnicities but shared the same condition: Everyone was poor.

Our first apartment had a swamp-green shag carpet with odors left behind by the past tenants. Then, an overflowed toilet lent the stench of sewage to the living room. The air conditioning broke in the hottest months of summer. The roaches got meaner and mightier with each spray of Raid. We lasted six months before we had to move again. We didn't move far. We could only afford another cheap apartment across the street. This one had the same shag carpet but in a cleaner orange shade. The air conditioning worked, and the roaches only came out at night.

On the weekends, Dad did yardwork to earn extra money for another baby due after the birth of the last one, a year earlier. He came home in the evenings, drenched in sweat from the brutal humid heat. His arms, neck, and face were burnt from the sun and scratched from tree branches and bushes. He didn't mind; he preferred this labor to clearing the jungles of Vietnam. No matter how tough the job, Dad was grateful that he worked of his own free will.

My parents had not planned on a fourth child so soon, but as with everything unexpected thrown their way, the two of them pressed on. Dad, as part of a yard crew, mowed and trimmed as many lawns as he could to earn less than fifty dollars at the end of the day. Diapers and baby formula ate up the extra money fast.

Mom worked in a company that assembled mini blinds. For eight hours at a stretch, she stood on the factory floor threading pieces of blinds into long strings to form shades for six-foot-tall windows. In a day, she had to finish at least thirty mini blinds and box them for delivery. Mom endured the long hours of standing and lifting, despite her pregnancy.

Mom continued to work until she had to be hospital- ized in the last trimester for fever and nonstop vomiting. She spent several days hooked up to an IV pole. She had no appetite; the smell and sight of food made her nauseated. She rubbed her belly and prayed for the baby while she lay in the hospital bed.

Dad hustled from work to the hospital to home, check- ing on Mom and us children. We had no family or friends close enough to ask for help. He became good at preparing baby bottles and changing diapers. Dad even taught Van and me how to care for our baby sister, Thanh, who had just turned one.

When the hospital discharged Mom, her petite frame had shrunk from weight loss. The fear and guilt she felt for her baby gnawed at her. Mom returned to work less than a week after her hospital discharge, despite Dad's urging her to stay home. She knew the family needed her income to survive.

Exactly seven days before Christmas, Dad rushed Mom to the county hospital where she delivered their last child, a baby girl. Everyone in the family hoped for a boy, but we soon realized that this baby was an early Christmas gift and lifelong treasure for our family. Mom named the baby To, meaning "cherished one." Dad, however, gave her the nickname of "Little Hen" because she was born in the Lunar New Year of the Rooster. She had a sprinkle of soft fine hair that stood straight up, like a rooster's comb. We would later learn that she lived up to her nickname by being the first in the family to wake up every morning. She was alert like a rooster but never made much noise. The baby had a sweet temperament to match her constant smiling face. She rarely cried even when she was hungry, soiled, or sick. It was almost as if she sensed our family's disadvantages and didn't want to burden us. We bundled the baby in a soft blanket woven by one of Mom's coworkers. Little Hen came home on an unusually cold Texas December day.

From the start, Mom's maternal intuition told her that something was different about Little Hen. She kept watch as the weeks passed. Yet, Mom's time and attention were also pulled by three other children and her work. She only had two weeks' maternity leave. Her body, exhausted from childbirth and caring for three children, yearned for rest. But Mom knew that she could be easily replaced at the factory, so she had to persevere.

In the following months, Mom noticed more physical differences in her infant. Little Hen had a thick fold of skin over her eyelids that caused her to lift her entire head when she wanted to look up. She was slow to sit and crawl. My parents thought they just needed to be patient. The baby's plump rosy cheeks and lips put their concerns at ease, temporarily.

MOM CAME HOME AT the end of her day shift and found Dad holding the limp baby on his shoulder instead of getting ready to start his night shift. Without money for childcare, my parents worked different shifts.

"She's been vomiting all day," he told Mom.

The baby tried to open her eyes at the sound of Mom's voice but did not give the normal lovable smile. When she stopped smiling, we knew something was wrong. My parents took her to the emergency room where the doctors decided to admit the listless baby into the hospital.

My parents waited for the doctors to give them news on Little Hen. The cold temperature inside the hospital and heavy smell of disinfectant made Dad feel sick. The fear for his youngest magnified his trepidation. Dad brought Van and me along to help translate. We were still in the second and third grade, but with the births of two additional siblings in quick succession, we assumed more responsibilities.

Two doctors came to the lobby where we waited. The doctors dispensed a long explanation that my parents could not understand. My brother and I heard the words but did not grasp the message or know the Vietnamese words to explain to our parents. We were caught between two worlds and not equipped at that age to navigate both. The doctors tried again. They explained that the baby received IV medication to help her with hydration and vomiting. They expected her to improve.

But then they used words like "special needs" and expressed a concern for "mental retardation," an acceptable term at the time, based on the baby's developmental history. I did not understand. I heard the word "retarded" used in school when the kids were mean to each other. I was confused and scared to think the word applied to my baby sister. The doctors finally found an adult Vietnamese translator who broke the news that the baby might have an intellectual developmental disability. The news confirmed my parents' suspicion, but it was still a blow to us all.

After the sobering talk, we went to visit the baby who was lying in her hospital bed. Her soft head of hair was shaved, and a bandage covered the IV site on her scalp where saline flowed from the IV tubing.

"Hey, Little Hen," Dad said. She looked up and gave him the familiar endearing smile that melted his heart.

Dad looked over at Mom, whose eyes brimmed over with tears. She felt guilt and blamed herself. She believed her illness might have caused her daughter's condition. Dad shared Mom's sorrow. He also felt overwhelmed and lost. He thought escaping Vietnam would allow his children a better future. Now, he felt that his youngest daughter's future was sealed with disadvantages beyond anyone's control. He took a deep breath and realized that if she was meant to have this unfortunate fate, it was better that she was born in America than in Vietnam. He stroked the baby's soft cheeks with his calloused fingers.

WHEN MY PARENTS SWITCHED to daytime shifts, they had to leave for work at an early hour before anyone in the apartment complex would agree to babysit. They needed me to take the babies to the home of a Cuban woman who lived a few doors from us before leaving for school. I took on the role at nine years old, when the babies were three and two.

In the morning before I headed for school, I woke my sisters and dressed them with the clothes that Mom laid out. I carried Little Hen in one arm and with the other arm I hauled the diaper bag, along with my own school bag. My sister, Thanh, still a toddler, scurried behind as the three of us headed to the babysitter's home.

School no longer constituted a dreaded place for me. Most mornings started off well with the free breakfast Van and I received. The smell of cooked sausage and blueberry muffins coming from the cafeteria, on some mornings, meant they were serving my favorite breakfast. The school provided a free breakfast and lunch for families at the poverty level. It was the only government help our father would accept.

With each setback in life, Dad experienced quiet little victories that gave him purpose and pushed him to move forward. He even noticed a change in my attitude toward school. For a while, he had worried that I would give up. Then one day, on coming home from work, he saw me sitting on the couch reading to my little sisters. The babies snuggled their heads against my shoulders as I read to them simple word books I found in the library. I stumbled and struggled to sound out every other word as I read, but my two little audience members didn't seem to mind.

Shortly after we had arrived in Texas, Dad had enrolled me in second grade and Van in third grade. Texas had an ESL (English as a second or foreign language) program, but by then we no longer needed ESL. Regardless, we fell behind our peers. The school placed us in a special curriculum along with other students who were behind.

Dad was curious when he saw me bring home different picture books every day to read. "Another new book today?" he asked.

"Mrs. Hamilton has a reading contest for the student who reads the most books in her class. After I read a book, I have to write five sentences about it. The winner gets a prize at the end of the year." I wanted to tell him that the letters and numbers were starting to make sense and I didn't feel as dumb as I believed I was.

I also didn't know how to explain to him that I saw how hard he and Mom worked and how I wanted to help them someday. Instead, I looked back down at my book and continued reading.

On the last day of school, Mrs. Hamilton announced to the class that I won the prize for reading the most books for the school year. She presented me with a small brown teddy bear, which to my child's eyes was more precious than any jeweled trophy. I couldn't wait to show it to my parents.

I tucked my prize away in a brown paper bag that contained my school supplies and miscellaneous items inside my desk to take home for the summer. I walked home with both arms encircling the paper bag, protecting the teddy bear inside. I emptied the paper bag on the carpet floor at home, and out spilled pencils and crayons, but no teddy bear. I shook the empty bag and saw the gaping hole at the bottom. I ran outside and retraced my path from home to school but did not find the teddy bear. It was lost. I cried for the rest of the day.

Dad tried to console me. He promised to buy me a new teddy bear, but I only wanted the one that I earned. After supper, Dad found me sitting in a corner of the bedroom I shared with my siblings, trying to read an advertisement magazine I found in the mail and my eyes still puffy from crying. He sat down next to me and said, "The true prize was the improvement in your reading and writing skills from all those books you read. That is something you can never lose. And there will be bigger rewards in your future from it."

Dad looked around the cramped apartment and noticed an old hula hoop next to a partially deflated red rubber ball that my brother and I used for games of dodgeball with the neighborhood kids. He knew we seldom asked for new toys, but he wished he could give us what his father had provided for him.

Dad found frugal ways for us to enjoy family time. During summer camping trips in Galveston, an island off the southeast coast of Texas, fifty miles from Houston,

Dad taught my brother and me how to catch crab. The twenty-seven-mile-long island, with its tan, sandy beaches, faces the Gulf of Mexico.

We headed to the island to be near the water during the blistering hot months of Texas summer and because Dad heard about the crabbing on Galveston. Ever since his first attempt at catching the crustaceans in Maryland, he was hooked. Dad packed the tent, a cooler, and some pots and pans into the back of the station wagon. Then we'd hit the interstate, going south toward Galveston. We found a campsite with an ocean view and pitched our tent. After our family settled into the campground, Dad went searching for the marsh and rocky pier suggested by his friends for the best crabbing. He usually took Van and me along while Mom stayed behind with the two younger children. Van and I couldn't decide which we liked more, catching the crabs or eating them.

"There is a skill and technique to crabbing that requires patience and strategy," Dad said while holding a string tied to a chicken thigh. He threw the chicken part into the water and we watched it sink to the bottom. After several minutes, a small circle of oily film formed on the surface around the bait, and we saw a slight tug on the string. Van and I jumped with excitement, knowing we had a bite.

My brother and I learned from Dad's technique and soon netted one crab after another until we filled up the ice chest. The activity required concentration and adroit eye–hand coordination. We didn't need fancy video games, which in the early to mid-'80s consisted of Atari games like Pac-Man and Tetris. We had more fun crabbing. With a cooler filled with the blue gulf crustaceans, we headed back to the campground for a crab boil.

When my siblings and I were asleep in the tent, Dad sat outside with Mom, stoking the fire pit. The calm silence of nighttime relaxed them. In their quiet conversation, they pondered about the future and their finances. Then Mom reminded Dad about the Vietnamese insurance salesman they recently met through friends who wanted to sell them a policy that combined life insurance and retirement in one. They did not have any money saved and still lived paycheck to paycheck, but they had steady work. Dad worked at Compaq Computers, where he felt happy and secure with his job. Mom worked as a custodian in a school district not too far from home.

"He seems like a nice man," Mom noted. "He said we only needed to pay the premium for seven years, and we would be guaranteed a retirement fund. If anything happened to either one of us, the children would be taken care of."

"We would need an extra two hundred dollars a month to pay the policy premium," Dad said. "Our largest expense now is rent."

"We could do what the salesman suggested and move into the trailer he wants to sell us. It's cheap and we could use the extra money left for rent to pay the premium," Mom suggested.

Dad ruminated over the idea as he watched the embers refusing to die in the diminishing fire. The burnt wood glowed on stubbornly.

"Let's do it!" Dad agreed.

It seemed like a good idea, until they saw the trailer.

A pale yellow, rusty metal box about seventy feet long and fifteen feet wide, with patches of large sheet metal tacked on the outside from haphazard repair jobs, sat by itself in a field with waist-high grass. An old refrigerator, an oven, and a chipped toilet lay scattered several feet from the back of the trailer, likely the site of a dumping ground at one point. The only other structure nearby, less than a hundred feet from the trailer, was a t-shirt printing warehouse that had one car parked in front.

The poor lighting inside the dark trailer could not conceal its age. Everywhere, there were signs that the trailer needed to go to the dump like the discarded toilet and fridge that sat outside. The faded flowered wallpaper peeled at its edges, waiting for someone to rip it off. Holes and cracks in the corners shot warm air and light into the musty trailer. Critters of all kinds could sneak their way inside. There was no central heating or air conditioning. The one window AC in the living room blew weak air, not enough to cool even a small corner.

The trailer's conditions depressed my parents, but they decided to push forward. Before the move-in date, they spent weekends making repairs to our new home. Dad installed a new AC window unit in the master bedroom and the living room. They pulled out the smelly old carpet and replaced it with a less-used carpet that they got at a discount. They went to an estate sale and purchased used furniture at a bargain price. The estate even threw in a few free business suits, styled for the 1970s, from the deceased owner. After several weeks of patchwork, the dwelling was still a disaster, but they decided that it would be home for the time being. "We've lived in far worse conditions during our refugee days," Dad said to us when we all stood in front of our new home on move-in day.

At my old school, I did not feel different from my classmates. But starting junior high at the new school, I began to feel conspicuous in clothes from thrift shops and church donations. I discovered that my new classmates had few wants unmet. Every day, I sat on the school bus watching the manicured neighborhoods with their rows of grand brick homes fly past. The school bus dropped off the other kids before making its last stop near my home on the outer perimeter of the school district. The school bus would not drive into the area where the trailer was parked. Van and I had to walk half a mile out to the main street, where the bus picked us up and dropped us off.

On the walk home, I trailed behind my brother, lost in my own thoughts. I dreamed of a better future for myself and my family. I wanted to someday buy my parents a new car and a new pair of shoes for my dad. I remembered my father's advice. He told me, "Work hard now in school so that you won't have to work harder later in life like me and your mom—unless it's a passion that you want to follow. But then, that would be by choice, and it won't feel like work."

I took his guidance to heart and, in elementary school, worked my way up from reading and writing below grade level to finally catching up. I had a new motivation at the new school: to work even harder. I wanted to prove, mostly to myself, that disadvantages did not define self-worth.

Even the hardships we had endured as refugees, under the most deprived conditions, did not make living in the trailer easier. During the summer, we melted from the heat. The small window AC units did little to cool the trailer during the hottest summer months.

In the peak hours of heat, Dad sprayed the trailer roof with water to cool it down. Most of the time it felt like living inside a boiling tin can. The two babies soaked in sweat, and their cheeks turned bright red from the summer heat.

Houston seemed to have only one season—summer—and a few cold days in winter. But during the two years we lived in the trailer, it felt like a transition from the jungles to the Arctic. Without central heating, we used two small space heaters to keep warm during those frigid months. However, they did little to keep the cold drafts out. Holes and cracks throughout the trailer allowed bitter winter air in and invited large field rats to squeeze their way into our home. During the coldest winter nights, the entire family huddled in the master bedroom with all space heaters cranked to maximum heat. In the winter mornings, Van and I warmed our school clothes and socks in front of the space heater and dreaded coming home. It was so frigid inside that we could see the white mist of warm air from our nostrils and mouths when we breathed or talked. We kept our winter coats on while inside the trailer.

Besides the trailer falling apart, the faithful blue station wagon, having racked up over 300,000 miles and taken us across ten states, was on its last legs. It finally gave out when the transmission broke and would not go into reverse. Dad did not have the money to get the transmission fixed. He had to carefully plan where to park so that he would not have to reverse the car. When he was stuck and couldn't wiggle his way out of a tight spot, he'd put the station wagon in neutral, then jump out and push the car backward. Even when he finally saved enough money for another used car, he did not want to let go of his blue four-wheeled friend.

It was like saying goodbye to a family member when the tow truck came to haul the old station wagon to the junkyard. My siblings and I lined up outside the trailer and stood with Dad as a mainstay in our lives was pulled away. We watched in silence and kept our eyes glued to its blue silhouette until it disappeared from sight.

After the departure of his station wagon, Dad had no problem parting with the trailer. My siblings and I jumped with joy at the decision to move out of the dilapidated metal box where we had spent two freezing winters and two sweltering summers. As for the investment on the insurance policy, it turned out to be a costly lesson. My parents did not know about the fine print regarding the changing premium rates and could not keep up with the payments. They lost all the money put into the insurance policy and supposed retirement plan.

Living in the trailer was another rock-bottom episode we survived. But the real lesson came from the faithful

Ford station wagon. It gave us a final message before it left. It reminded us that there was only one direction that we could go: forward!

CHAPTER 21

The Reagan Letter

"THE WATER IS A unique blue, almost a crystal blue," Dad observed as the van drove across the bridge to Key Largo, the first in a chain of islands to Key West. The sun, high in the soft blue sky, reflected off the calm water, giving it a gleaming silver luster on that summer day in 2015.

"A jade blue," Mom amended.

"A Key West blue. We're almost there," Cousin Hung said, while keeping his foot steady on the gas pedal.

General Di chuckled. "I agree with all your shades of blue."

Souvenir shops peppered the island, offering wood carvings of pink flamingos and giant seashell signs waving at passing motorists to stop and rummage inside for trinkets. One shop in particular caught Mom's attention.

"Let's stop up ahead," she suggested, pointing to a café with a sign that advertised all things made from Key limes: pies, cakes, candies, sauces, skin care, and tourist baubles. We wandered inside and smelled the zesty scent of fresh citrus and vanilla.

Half of the store sold souvenirs, and the other half indulged the customer's sweet tooth. We sat down at a table with an old-fashioned red-and-white checkered tablecloth and ordered the renowned Key lime pie. Our group stared with interest when the waitress brought out the pale-yellow custard pastry with clouds of whipped cream. The desserts most of the group (myself excepted) favored and grew up eating contained natural ingredients with little sugar, like steamed sticky rice infused with coconut milk wrapped in banana leaves. Our lips initially puckered from the tartness on the first bite, but the sugariness soon mellowed the crispy bite of the lime.

Halfway through our pie, Dad and the others scattered to look around the store. Only General Di and I stayed behind to finish the pie.

"How did you like being in the US Army?" General Di asked.

"It was one of the best experiences of my life," I said. "I think the experience also depends on what you make of it." General Di nodded with his ever-present smile.

When the last crumb of pie was polished off our plates, General Di took a paper napkin and wrote down a word. He delighted in learning new English terms, which filled the pages of the palm-sized notebook he carried around with him. He handed the napkin to me and said, "This word best expresses my feelings about meeting you."

I looked at the napkin with the word "invaluable" scribbled across. I carefully folded the napkin and tucked it in my wallet. It was one of the best compliments I ever received.

A LITTLE OVER FIVE years into their imprisonment, General Di and his fellow internees received news
from their families that the US had elected a new president.
The historic inauguration of Ronald Reagan in 1981 did
not escape the attention of the political prisoners kept hidden from the world in the jungles of North Vietnam.

"We should write to President Reagan and ask for his help.
He hates communism and should know about us—rotting
in this hell on earth! What do you think?" General Dao
asked. General Di agreed, but he fretted that this move carried the highest risk and could mean death for all involved
if caught.

"My family will help. I will ask them to smuggle in paper
and pen and get the letter out," General Dao continued.

Over the following months, the two men, along with a
group of trusted officers, worked on the letter. They elected
General Di to write while each contributed their ideas.
The officers took turns huddling in groups of twos and
threes and whispered their thoughts to General Di while
they worked in the field planting rice and potatoes for the
communists. During their evening breaks, they continued
the discussion in secret. Generals Di and Dao collected
the comments and reviewed them together, whispering at
night in the dark cell when the guards left.

In the early dawn, when just enough light poured through
the dingy prison windows above his cell, General Di pulled
out the precious pieces of paper and pen. In careful, neat
penmanship, he composed the letter to President Reagan.
General Dao sat by his side while the other prisoners in
the cell kept watch for approaching guards. General Di
and General Dao scrutinized each phrase, wrestling with
how to express it in a language that was not their native
tongue. General Di made sure to convey his own feelings
of gratitude to the American people for sacrificing their
sons and daughters in the aid of South Vietnam's fight for

democracy. This activity went on for months, piecemeal, until the authors were satisfied with the result.

When General Di completed the letter's last sentence, he looked it over a dozen times more and hoped that it communicated the message of those imprisoned. He finalized the document with a strong deliberate signature followed by his rank and last assignment. The other signees followed suit and sealed their involvement with a signature. Each signatory knew that by putting their name on the document, they marked themselves for execution should the letter fall into communist hands.

The letter read:

North Vietnam January 21, 1981

To Mr. R. Reagan
President of the United States of America

Dear Mr. President,

We are addressing you, from this sinister concentration camp, our warm greetings at your entering . . . office.

Today, when you make the oath to assume the reins of government as the fortieth President of the United States of America, we have been sustaining five years and a half in this dismal communist prison—years of exhausting hard labor and starvation and harsh deprivation as well as unending mental torture with an unlimited time ahead.

Despite of [sic] the everlasting agony we have stood fast; held to the high ideals for liberty, of anti-communism and never lost trust in the United States, prominent leader in these noble causes.

We resolutely believe that the United States who promising [sic] an unselfish and elevated aim in South Viet Nam by using these precious resources and ultimately sending their beloved, gallant sons fighting side by side [with] us for many years to support our country in his safeguarding his [sic] *freedom, will never leave us to the mercy of the communist tyrants.*

We are field grade and general officers who fought at the frontline without failure till the end, in April 1975. We accepted to share the misery of captivity beside our comrades-in-arms. On behalf of hundreds of thousands of South Vietnamese prisoners, both servicemen and civilians—ranging from privates to general officers, from hamlet chiefs to prime minister, not excluding priests of Christian and Buddhist faiths, members of anti-communist political parties—we are sending you this message of faith and hope.

In the cold dark cells of the condemned ward, overcoming innumerable difficulties, closely we kept track of your election campaign. By choosing you as his President, the American people fully conscious of his great worldwide trust, entirely aware the threat of the despotic and bloodthirsty communist regime—the plague of humankind—has shown his steady determination to meet the challenge, to lead the free world in the fight for freedom and democracy and to prevail. As regards us, we understand you—a symbol of resolute and consistent ideal of anticommunism—as hope, new hope, for our freedom.

Yours faithfully,

MAJOR GENERAL TRAN BA DI, DEPUTY COMMANDER, IV CORPS (1973–1975)

MAJOR GENERAL LE MINH DAO, COMMANDING GENERAL, 18TH INFANTRY DIVISION (1972–1975)

BRIGADIER GENERAL HUYNH VAN LAC, COMMANDING GENERAL, 9TH INFANTRY DIVISION (1973–1975)

COLONEL NGO VAN MINH, CHIEF OF STAFF, III CORPS

COLONEL NGUYEN THANH CHUAN,
COMMANDING OFFICER, 101ST RANGER
DIVISION

COLONEL NGO KY DUNG, COMMANDER, 2ND
REGIMENT, 18TH INFANTRY DIVISION

COLONEL LE XUAN HIEU, COMMANDER, 43RD
REGIMENT, 18TH INFANTRY DIVISION

GENERAL DAO SECURED THE letter inside his waistband in case the guards should check his pockets during the family visit. His heart raced, but he managed to maintain a calm exterior. When the guards looked away, he slipped the letter to his sister. General Dao's pulse kept soaring even after he returned to his cell. He waited and prayed, feeling dizzy and nauseated, while the guards searched his sister on her exit from the jail. He knew that getting the letter out of prison was just the first obstacle in a dangerous passage to the White House.

General Dao's sister managed to leave the prison and make her way back to Saigon without getting caught. But travel in postwar Vietnam was met with frequent and, sometimes, unexpected stop-and-search inspections by the communists. Once the letter arrived in Saigon undetected, General Dao's family sent it on to relatives in Paris. They could not send it directly to the US for fear of attracting communist attention. Any international mail fell under suspicion and was subjected to inspection. The letter arrived in Paris untampered. Once it left Vietnam, General Dao's family could breathe a sigh of relief. From Paris, the letter traveled to relatives in Washington, DC.

When the letter reached American soil, it had to find its way into the Oval Office. General Dao's kin sought out ARVN Lieutenant General Ngo Quang Truong, the IV Corps commander in the Mekong Delta during part of the war. General Truong fled Vietnam during the fall of

General Di's fellow prisoners elect him to write a letter to President Ronald Reagan shortly after the latter takes office in 1981. (Courtesy of General Di's family)

Saigon and settled in Virginia. General Truong reached out to Lieutenant General John Cushman, who contacted a Reagan staff member, Lieutenant Colonel Richard T. Childress, who was the Asian Affairs Director from 1981 to 1988. Childress had also been an American advisor who knew General Dao during the war.

"It is him!" Childress exclaimed when he recognized General Dao's signature. The two reunited years later, and General Dao disclosed to Childress the letter's odyssey. He did not feel the need to ask Childress if the letter made its way to the desk of President Reagan. It was enough for General Dao to know that the letter had miraculously made it as far as it had.

In the last month of President Reagan's final term in office, his administration worked out an agreement with Vietnam's communist government that all ARVN soldiers and officers held in the prison camps be freed and allowed to immigrate to the US. In 1987, President Reagan sent retired Army Vice Chief of Staff and former Chairman of the Joint Chiefs of Staff General John Vessey Jr. to Vietnam to account for Americans missing in action and to push for the release of South Vietnamese leaders. The effort to pressure the Vietnamese government to release the political prisoners of war continued with President George H. Bush's administration.

As the letter made its way to President Reagan, the internees in North Vietnam's concentration camp waited with hope. It gave them a sense of purpose and temporarily took their minds away from their sorrow and suffering. General Dao encouraged his cellmates, "The mere fact that we have accomplished such a feat without discovery is a victory!"

Over twenty years later, General Dao's sister hand delivered a copy of the letter to General Di's family in Orlando. The fate of the original letter was unknown. But the copy found a home with General Di's family.

CHAPTER 22

Seventeen Years

QUE HUONG, GENERAL DI'S daughter, sat alone in her room and addressed her letters to Amnesty International, the Red Cross, and Vietnam's communist government. A once bubbly girl of eighteen with dimpled cheeks and a wide smile like her father's, Que Huong became quiet and withdrawn in her new home in America. She didn't want to talk to anyone since the day her family fled Vietnam. She just wanted to be left alone with her letters. The outwardly quiet and shy girl had a steadfast passion to free her father. Que Huong began a relentless letter-writing campaign once her family settled in Orlando in 1976 after learning that he was still alive from a *Time* magazine article published the same year showing her father's picture in the concentration camp. She wrote to whomever would listen and still wrote when no one answered.

Que Huong's personal crusade gave her purpose to battle the culture shock, change of fortune, and loneliness without her father. The family, once privileged with cooks and maids, had to scratch out their own means of survival during the early years in America. The family of five settled into a small two-bedroom apartment in Orlando. Mrs. Di found work as a seamstress. Que Huong and her brothers went to work on farms and in restaurant kitchens while attending school. Yet, the hardest part of life for the family was not the poverty but the feeling of isolation. Orlando did not have a Vietnamese community or a large Asian population in the late seventies. Their lack of English compounded the loneliness. Que Huong's letters took her away from the despair and brought her the hope of seeing her father again.

Que Huong had an ally in her mission to free her father, retired Army Colonel Douglas P. Harper. One of General Di's last messages to his family on the telephone call at the airport before they flew out of Vietnam was to contact Colonel Harper once they reached America. Colonel Harper came to visit them at Camp Pendleton, where they stayed for the first few months before settling in Orlando. He remained in contact with General Di's family and wrote to Congress urging for his friend's release. For each letter that he wrote, he sent a copy to General Di's family.

FROM 1976 TO 1988, the communist authorities transferred General Di from one remote northern prison to the next: Yen Bai, Ha Tay, and Nam Ha. Over time, the compound at Nam Ha grew into a series of single-story stone buildings with gabled roofs covered with corrugated tin, enclosed by a barbed-wire fence. The early years of hard labor in the wilderness became an indelible memory, but the mental torture and deprivation remained a constant punishment.

The gradual release of most captives made General Di believe that he might spend his remaining years languishing and forgotten. The prison, once packed with hundreds of political inmates, dwindled to a few dozen visible prisoners. By 1985, only three internment camps remained in North Vietnam: Tan Ky, Thanh Cam, and Nam Ha. Then in1988, the communists whisked General Di over one thousand miles from North Vietnam back to the south, where he spent the next four years along with his three cellmates locked away at Ham Tan prison camp.

In the seventeenth year of his prison sentence, General Di noticed a change in treatment from his captors. He and his fellow inmates were given more freedom to roam the grounds outside their prison, with minimal supervision. One spring morning in 1992, on a walk foraging for edible plants and wildlife for their meal, General Dao revealed to General Di his prediction that their release would soon come. They surmised that the fake act of civility was merely a hollow attempt by the communist cadre to ameliorate the years of brutality. General Dao stated, "They don't want us to leave here and let the world know of their savagery!"

After seventeen years and five days, the guards came into the cell that contained the last four imprisoned generals and told them to pack their belongings. They were going home.

"I cannot believe we are free from this hell on earth, Brothers!" General Dao exclaimed.

General Di sat stunned and a little suspicious, hoping this was not another twisted joke by his captors. The other generals shed cautious tears of joy. General Di said a quiet prayer of gratitude, nonetheless. Those prayers, from the first one that sounded in his mind on the first night of capture in 1975 to the countless ones he uttered with his cellmates and to himself through years of incarceration, consoled and sustained him.

On May 5, 1992, Major General Di, Major General Le Minh Dao, Brigadier General Do Ke Giai, and Brigadier General Le Van Than walked out of prison together after having served the longest recognized sentence among general officers. A car waited outside the fence, ready to take them home. At the gate, General Di took one final look at Ham Tan prison, the last physical reminder of a long nightmare.

Each mile away from the prison brought General Di more relief and made the release believable. He was anxious to see how much the world outside his prison cell had changed. When he reached Saigon, the beloved city of his youth, he found the former capital's name changed to Ho Chi Minh City. He saw that Vietnam had changed, but not progressed. The same alabaster-white concrete building that stood decades ago looked dingy and stained with dark streaks from smog and mildew. The city, too poor to erect new buildings, continued to occupy what the generations before had left. Streets littered with trash and potholes seemed to carry more people on bicycles and fewer in automobiles. He saw more pedestrians in tattered clothes begging on the streets of Saigon than he had remembered during the war.

After 1975, the US imposed an economic sanction, refusing to trade with Vietnam. Other western countries followed and shunned Vietnam for its violation of human rights. The trade embargos threw Vietnam into an impoverished disaster.

Other than the news from the *Time* magazine article that Colonel Harper sent, Que Huong and her family received little information about her father's status. As the months and years drifted by, their hopes waned, but they remained vigilant.

Then, she got an unexpected call from General Le Minh Dao's daughter one day in 1992. She heard over the phone, "Our fathers will soon be released!"

Que Huong could not believe the news as a surge of emotions spilled over—happiness, relief, fear of disappointment, hope. She immediately contacted an uncle in Saigon to inform him of what she'd heard. She was not given the specific day of her father's release or if it would truly happen. Nonetheless, Que Huong gave her contact information to her uncle in case he received any update.

The next night, her uncle called back. He asked her, "Do you want to speak to your father?" Que Huong thought he was playing a joke on her or had just "lost his mind." She could not imagine the release to be that soon after receiving the news.

Then she heard her father's voice on the other end: "How are you, Daughter?"

It had been seventeen years since she had heard that voice. The passing years deepened the tone of his voice, but she recognized the warmth that her father exuded. Too stunned to respond, Que Huong remained silent. Then she let out a cry, followed by a storm of tears that had built up for almost half of her life.

He paused to let her cry. When she collected herself, he gave her the names of prisoners who were released with him and their family's contact information. He asked her to notify their families in America. She knew it was definitely her father at the other end—still warm and practical— just the way she remembered. He cared for others before himself. After speaking with her father, she contacted the State Department to let them know of his release. Without knowing details or the specifics behind her father's discharge from prison, Que Huong believed the US government had played a big part in his freedom.

Like all "reeducated" South Vietnamese, General Di experienced discrimination in the new communist society. He could not work to support himself. He had to report to his assigned probation officer every day. Travel outside his district required paperwork and approval from the authorities. Before the cellmates departed for their separate homes on their last day together, General Di said to them, "We have been released from a hard labor camp to a larger prison—Vietnam."

Soon after their release, all four generals applied to leave Vietnam through the Orderly Departure Program (ODP). Established by the UNHCR in 1979, this program allowed Vietnamese to leave their homeland and resettle in the United States in a safe and systematic way to avoid the desperate escapes previously attempted by the "boat people." Permission from the communist government to leave Vietnam was not easy to obtain, and General Di's paperwork was blocked several times. However, by 1992, communist Vietnam courted better relations with the United States.

Years of communism without free enterprise taught the communists that the doctrine they preached brought only poverty and stagnation to the country they captured. After continual pressure from organizations to support his release, General Di received permission from the communists to leave the country. Communist Vietnam ceased to be his home.

In April 1993, General Di boarded a flight from Vietnam to America to rejoin his family.

During the long flight across the Pacific Ocean, he let his mind wander in a rare moment since his capture. He pondered about the lives of his children who were now grown adults and he a much older man. He was imprisoned at the prime of his life, at age forty-four, and released at age sixty-one; his captors had stolen seventeen years from him and his family.

He did not want to hold on to regrets and bitterness. It was not his nature. The years of austerity trained him to shake off dark thoughts. He had to discipline his psyche to survive and not break. General Di shifted his focus to the hope of rebuilding his life.

He made a stop at the Stanford, California, home of his friend Colonel Harper before heading to his destination in Orlando. General Di found Colonel Harper's wife waiting for him, in her husband's place, at the airport. His loyal friend had passed away during his imprisonment. Colonel Harper did not get the opportunity to see his efforts realized, but his wife along with other American friends were there in his place. During the visit, the friends presented General Di with a thousand dollars to start his new life in America.

General Di, overwhelmed by their generosity, could not accept the gift. He told them, "I am grateful for your friendship. I do not want anything more. You are my American family."

After a brief visit, General Di boarded a flight to Orlando, Florida, where his family and supporters waited at the airport. When the plane touched down, General Di checked his watch and noted the time, but the date caused him to pause: April 30, 1993. A bittersweet smile crept on his face. He felt the pain of the day, the brothers in arms he had lost and the guilt for those still imprisoned. Yet, the joy of seeing his family again softened his grief. How ironic, he mused, that the arrival to his new home should fall on the anniversary of the loss of his native homeland.

General Di's family kept their gaze fixed at the gate. Then he walked out toward them. The thick, jet-black hair that they remembered had streaks of gray. The round, merry face had become weathered and lined from years of deprivation and punishment. He worried that they might not recognize him. But he could not miss the group waiting for him. Excitement and tears filled the eyes of his loved ones. It took him a few seconds to register that the adults in front of him were the children he last saw before he left for work on that April morning in 1975. They encircled him and embraced him. At that moment, he felt free.

CHAPTER 23

The American Dream

I WATCHED THE roadside convenient stores and condominiums blur together as we drove across Key Largo until I saw an aqua blue sign that caught my interest: John Pennekamp Coral Reef State Park. I wanted to see the coral reef, but hesitated, not wanting to delay our travel.

Cousin Hung noticed my glancing back at the sign. "Is there something that you want to see? We're on vacation, there's no hurry," the gracious host remarked. "Anyway, I need to pull over to refuel."

When Cousin Hung stopped at a gas station, I got out of the van, still gazing at the direction of the sign we just passed. I took out my phone to search the state park. I looked back and forth from my phone to the road.

"You look lost," a man with snow-white hair and mustache commented. I glanced up from my phone and gave him a smile.

"Do you know how to get to Pennekamp Park?" I asked.

"Sure do. I've lived here all my life. I'm a lobster fisherman. The park is on my way to the harbor. If you want to follow me, I'll lead you there."

Whether they liked it or not, I committed my crew for a visit to the aquatic park. We followed the local man in his pickup truck for several miles until we saw a sign that pointed us into the state park. He pulled alongside us and shouted, "I would invite you all to my boat, but I've got some lobster traps to set. Hope you enjoy your stay!" He waved and drove off.

"Such a nice man!" Mom said.

After paying the entrance fee, we drove along a winding path, shaded by a thick wooded area of native trees, featuring tropical hardwood hammocks and the familiar mangrove.

"These mangroves seem to follow me everywhere," Dad commented, remembering images of the pervasive trees of the Mekong Delta.

We drove up to a beach with palm trees and white sand. Everyone got out of the vehicle to explore. I drifted away from the group and walked alone on the beach. I saw water so clear that I could see to the bottom. I could smell the briny scent of sea and salt. Tiny fish swam by and burrowed into the seaweed. The sun's brilliant rays illuminated every crack and crevice of the sea floor.

I wandered to the side of the beach where black boulders covered with sea algae jutted out to the water. I became entranced, looking into the water like I had when I was five, but this was the Florida Keys, not Thailand. There were no crashing waves beating against stone boulders, just smooth water jiggling against the rocks like the calm tides of my family's lives since coming to America. I took a moment to appreciate the kindness my family found in neighbors and strangers, who

John Pennekamp Coral Reef State Park, Key Largo. From left to right: Cousin Hung and his wife, Hoang; Mom; me; "Little Hen"; Dad; General Di. (Courtesy of Tran B. Quan)

soothed the rough waters that we encountered as new immigrants.

There was no froth or foam in the water to distract me on that pristine beach at John Pennekamp Park like on the shores of Thailand. I stared into the clear water that day and understood the brave risks my parents took to escape their native country and their tenacity to keep forging ahead toward the American dream.

IN 1987, AFTER A two-year sentence in the trailer and at Mom's urging, Dad knew we needed a decent home. Our new weekend pastime became house hunting. Everyone packed into the new used family car, a sea-blue 1980 Chevy Malibu, and cruised the new neighborhoods that had popped up in Houston.

"I can build us another hut. How about a tree house?" Dad teased when my brother and I reminded Dad that we had lived in a hut, a motel, an apartment, and a trailer.

Visions of daily life played out in our minds with each new home we viewed. But the new home prices brought us back to reality. Undaunted, we scouted more homes until we discovered a brown ranch-style house in a modest neighborhood. Just like before with his trusted station wagon, Dad knew that the 1,700 square foot home, built in 1978, would be a match. He walked through each room and inspected the walls, carpet, and appliances; all appeared clean and in working condition. He went outside to examine the roof and backyard. He couldn't find any fault with the house, and we all liked it. Dad got it for $35,000—still a bargain in 1987.

Excitement kept everyone awake that first night in our new home. It felt like a return to civilization after living in the trailer that was parked in a desolate field. My siblings and I gathered in my parents' bedroom that night and asked if we could sleep there before we separated to our own rooms. We had to break the habit of squeezing together into the same room, a practice we acquired during the wintry nights in the trailer and our refugee days. We laid our blankets on the floor by our parents' bed, while Little Hen, who was almost six, snuggled between them. Dad's body ached from the lifting of boxes and furniture, but his mind was at peace and happy. He did not need to sleep to dream that night because his American dream had come true.

Dad's wish for a better life in the new home became reality in contented moments over the next several years. The baby of the family steadily got stronger and developed her own distinct personality. We saw Little Hen bloom into a funny, observant, and caring little girl. At the same time, Little Hen's physical impairment also became more obvious. Her arms and legs moved slower and weaker than those of kids her age, but that did not stop her eagerness to help. When given a task, she would not cease until the job

My parents give us a stable home. (Courtesy of Tran B. Quan)

was done. She struggled to tie her shoestrings at the age of ten, but she had an innate sense of dignity and emotional maturity beyond her years. When she sensed any one of us feeling down, without saying a word she would give us a hug.

Part of Dad's vision for the new home was family meals together. No matter how tight time and money became, my parents made sure that there was always a good Sunday family feast. In our early years in America, the staple of most meals consisted of rice, eggs, and packaged noodles. After they purchased the house, my parents spent more Sunday afternoons cooking together and improved their culinary skills.

While doing my homework, I could hear from the bedroom the sound of the cleaver chopping on the cutting board and the sizzling of meat frying in a hot pan. Soon, the warm aroma of fried chicken, fish, and traditional Vietnamese dishes like pho—a hearty noodle soup—floated through every room of the house.

Once the cooking was done, Dad sat back and watched us eat. He'd gauge our reaction to his Vietnamese American cuisine. When the food disappeared faster than he could plate it, he knew it was a hit. He discovered a satisfaction in cooking and feeding family, friends, neighbors, and anyone who stopped by the house.

Dad enjoyed hosting parties to show off his culinary creations. After the last guest left their supper party one night, he cleared the table while Mom started on the dishes. "Everyone seemed to enjoy the food," Mom said, sharing the same pride in their cooking.

"They suggested that we open up a place, maybe not a full restaurant. What do you think?" Dad asked casually, but it was an idea that he had chewed on for a while.

"We don't have any money to start up a business and we don't have the experience," Mom reminded him. This time, Dad was the dreamer and Mom brought him back to reality. The stable paychecks covered the mortgage and filled the home with food and friends. But there was not much left for savings after the bills were paid.

"We'll find a way to finance it," Dad insisted. "I know it's a risk, but we've taken so many risks already."

Mom paused, her mind churning. She had to admit her heart shared the same dream. She answered Dad with a smile and a glint of hope in her eyes. They had achieved the American dream of home ownership. Now they aimed for another piece of the American dream: free enterprise.

CHAPTER 24

N&T Seafood

MY PARENTS SCOURED THE Houston area for businesses ready to sell in 1992. They discovered several struggling, small seafood stores with owners ready to cut their losses. Dad figured that the only store he could afford had to be in the same condition as the trailer home. He found the trailer's business counterpart in a rough neighborhood of North Houston. The seafood market, an 800-square-foot building, sat on an island in the middle of an intersection surrounded by traffic. Chips in the blue paint over the outside sheet metal walls uncovered streaks of coppery rust that made the store look older than its four decades. It had passed through the hands of different owners who didn't have enough money for repairs or even demolition. The name "N&T Seafood" hung from a sign in a crooked slant outside the store. My parents didn't know what the initials stood for. They decided it was cheaper to just keep the name.

Within walking distance stood a mix of run-down apartment buildings, a neighborhood with homes just as old as and in similar disrepair to the store, and an elementary school a few blocks away. A police station located five miles up the street struggled to deter the crimes in the area. Although dangerous, the surrounding neighborhood had a sense of community. Everyone seemed to know each other's personal business, like who had just been incarcerated or who had just gotten out of jail.

It appeared that the store's dilapidation did not tempt many criminals to rob it. However, the burglar bars and bullet holes Dad counted in the front windows and walls revealed that it, too, had not been spared from crime. Dad did not change out the bullet-riddled windows. He thought they added character to the store—but mostly, he couldn't afford the repair.

Ten feet from the front door and the first thing that customers saw when they entered was a glass case where raw catfish, drum fish, trout, shrimp, and jars of oysters lay on a bed of ice. A plastic sign showing the menu stood above the glass case. The menu stretched across a thin plywood wall that separated the front from the back of the store. Customers had the option of ordering cooked items from the menu, selecting their own fish to be cleaned and cooked, or purchasing the raw seafood to take home.

The front half had three booths to seat customers. A floor fan stood at either end of the seating area to supplement the AC window unit. The back of the store was connected to a shed that had a table where Dad could clean and fillet the fish.

A few days before the grand opening, we came with mops, brooms, rags, and brushes to give the store a final cleaning. While Dad mopped the chipped tile floor, he could hardly believe that in a couple of days he would open his own business. It weighed on him that he was starting off the venture with nothing but a huge debt. He had to get loans from friends, relatives, banks, and credit cards.

Dad stayed up nights, worried and excited all at once. If the business failed, he could not imagine how he would ever pay off the loans. He and Mom both quit their jobs, which meant no steady income or health insurance for the family. His stomach ached from the risks, but Dad knew he had to give it a shot.

On a sunny, clear blue October day in 1992, my parents opened their first small business. They bought multicolored grand opening flags and strung them across the front of the store. My siblings and I used markers to draw homemade signs that advertised the daily specials, which we taped to the front windows.

A few cars with curious drivers stopped in front of the store to look at the posters advertising the day's special of three pieces of fish and three shrimp with side orders of french fries and a salad for $2.99. People sat in their cars looking at the store, then back at the sign, deciding whether to enter. Most drove off.

Behind the glass windows, Dad watched the cars pull away and wondered if the price was too high. His attention then turned to a man in a sleeveless white t-shirt on a bicycle, riding toward the store. *Probably someone from the neighborhood,* Dad thought. The man parked his bike and studied the homemade posters outside before entering.

"I only got two dollars; what can I get?" he demanded, slamming down the two bills on the counter.

"No problem. We give you the special: three fish, three shrimps. Special price for grand opening," Dad answered in broken English.

"Now you're talkin'. Fix me up!" the man smiled, showing his capped front gold tooth.

Then the phone rang with a takeout order, and three more customers came in. Mom ran to the kitchen to start cooking while Dad juggled the customer on the phone and the ones in the store. It was just the two of them on that day;

my siblings and I were in school, and my parents couldn't afford to hire any help. One customer ordered a plate of fried fish and shrimp while another wanted a fish fillet to take home. Dad weighed the fish, gave the order tickets to Mom, and raced to the back to clean the fish.

While they scrambled with the existing orders, another customer walked in and banged on the counter for service. Mom washed her hands, dried them on her apron, and ran to the front. Halfway through taking the customer's order, she sniffed burnt cornmeal batter and ran back to the kitchen to lift the shriveled fish out of the fryer. She had to start over. Customers in the front started yelling to the back kitchen that they needed to get back to work. The woman who ordered the fish fillet hollered, "What's taking so long? Did y'all have to go catch the fish?"

Dad dashed out to the front with a plastic bag containing his first sold filleted fish in hand and an apron covered with scales and splattered fish guts. He proudly lifted the plastic bag to show his handiwork. The woman snatched the bag of fish, held it up for inspection, and gave Dad a scowl. Dad had spent ten minutes scaling, gutting, washing, filleting, then chopping the fish into the size the customer wanted—all for merchandise sold for less than five dollars. He did not charge for the cleaning or filleting service.

Customers came into the market in frantic waves, followed by hours of silence. A few more trickled in before closing time. At the end of the first day, Dad counted less than two hundred dollars, minus the loss from several phone-in orders that never got picked up. When he subtracted the cost of supplies and the daily business expenditures, the amount earned that first day yielded a loss. Undaunted, Dad locked up the store and started his new ritual of sweeping, mopping, and taking out the garbage while Mom put away the food and washed the cutting boards and utensils.

Dad's American dream, N&T Seafood, on a traffic island in a rough Houston neighborhood. (Courtesy of Tran B. Quan)

They drove home that night with fish scales in their hair, cooking grease on their skin, and the stink of fish and sweat on their bodies. Their arms, legs, and backs ached, but they looked forward to the next business day.

Our family-operated endeavor meant that every member in the family worked. The store was open six days a week. When my parents launched the family business, Van and I started college locally. On some weekdays, I worked a few hours at the shop then went home to care for my two sisters, who were still in elementary school.

On weekends and in the summer, my little sisters came along to help box the orders while Van and I ran the front of the store. We darted from the front to the back to help with the cooking. At other times, we would hurry to the shed in the back to hand Dad a fish for cleaning.

We watched him run the fish scaler from the tail to the fish's head, scraping away, tiny silver scales flying in all directions. Then he took a knife with a long thin blade and sliced the meat away from the fish bone. With a cleaver, he chopped off the fish head and bagged it for customers who wanted to make soup stock from it. He scooped the fillet pieces into a basket and rinsed them thoroughly. During the entire time, a burning cigarette hung from the side of his mouth. Dad handed the cleaned fish to me or one of my siblings, which we would either take to the kitchen for Mom to cook or pack on ice for customers to take home. When he finished a job, Dad would take the last puff from his cigarette and smother the butt in a tin can that sat on the cement floor.

"Dad! It's not healthy!" we all fussed at him.

Dad answered back, "Not to worry. I would not let a speck of ash fall on my handiwork. Besides, no germ can survive the deep fryer."

After closing and cleaning the store, Mom and Dad usually did not make it home until well past eleven most nights. They worked through holidays and weekends. My parents did not mind that, while they fed others, they went hungry.

As business picked up, Fridays and Saturdays became the busiest days of the week, especially during Lent season. A line of customers extended outside the store on some Fridays. The phone rang continuously with call-in orders. The kitchen bustled with the sound of fish frying. Dad ran back and forth, cleaning the fish in the back and frying his rice on the wok. My siblings and I took customer orders and packed to-go boxes at a furious pace. But we still heard people jeer, "What's taking so long? Y'all need some help back there!"

Our family worked together in a synchronized rhythm most of the time. But when business became overwhelmingly busy, the stress levels rose along with the temperature in the kitchen. My parents' tempers flared, orders got confused, and a roomful of impatient customers stood waiting in the front. From the back, Dad could hear customers heckling, "Y'all need to quit fussin' back there and hurry up with my food!"

IN THE FIRST YEAR, the locals did not know what to make of my family. Most of the neighborhood customers wagered that the store would close after the first year, from either financial failure or fear of the area. We had to endure the initial hazing period. There were customers who refused to pay, customers who threatened to call the health department when they did not get their way, prank calls, and counterfeit money. The storefront windows were smashed. Gang graffiti covered the back and side walls of the store. Even the neighborhood kids made life difficult for us. They swarmed in after school, screaming and hollering disrespectful taunts and demands for soft drinks and french fries. Afterwards, they left a trail of ketchup and fries on the floor and counter. Once, when Dad caught some of them making the mess, they stuck out their tongues and ran out the door.

One afternoon, when the AC could not keep up with the stifling Texas heat and the back kitchen with its two blazing deep fryers roaring, the N&T owners reached their boiling point. In walked trouble, one of the young street entrepreneurs Mom recognized.

"Ay!" He yelled to get attention and slammed his fist on the counter several times. Dad was in the back, cleaning fish, while Mom was by the deep fryer in the kitchen. "Someone take my order!"

Mom came running out. "What you need?" she asked in her thick Vietnamese accent.

"I want the catfish special. Make it extra spicy. I want extra ketchup and tartar sauce. I want it extra crispy, but don't take too long," he demanded.

Mom went to the kitchen to start on his order. Before she dropped the battered catfish into the deep fryer, she heard another bang on the counter.

"My bad. I want to change my order to the trout special," he said.

"I start on your order already. Okay, I change it this time only," Mom said, feeling her annoyance grow.

Ten minutes later, Mom handed the young man the Styrofoam box with his cooked order inside. He opened it and felt the hot steam of fresh cooked food hit his face. He took a seat at the booth and drowned his food with Sriracha chili sauce before tasting it. Not a peep came from him while he devoured his food. When he polished the last crumb from his box, he closed the lid and approached Mom at the counter.

"I want my money back. It was too spicy," he said.

"You eat all your food. Now, you want money back?" Mom asked, feeling the vein on her temple throb.

"You gonna give me my money back, or you want me to call the health department?" the young thug threatened.

Hearing the commotion, Dad came out with his fish scaler in hand.

"Okay, young man, you call the health department, and I call the police," Dad warned.

"Man, give me my money back!" The thug raised his voice. Mom opened the cash register and pulled out five dollars.

She said, "You no good!"

He yanked the bill from her hand. A screaming match between Mom and the thug ensued. Dad grabbed a nearby broom and pointed the end toward the door to gesture him out. The thug shoved the door open and yelled profanity on his way out. Mom ran to the kitchen looking for the container of salt. She threw a handful of salt behind the thug as if she were warding off evil spirits. The thug turned around and gave her a half scared and half confused look.

The next day, the same thug returned. This time, he came in looking abashed and gave Mom a wide smile. He ordered his food like a gentleman and ate it in the store without a peep. He became a regular, faithful customer at N&T Seafood and a defender to Mom whenever he saw someone give her trouble.

THE SHOP DID NOT make much profit in the first few years. Bills accumulated, but my parents managed to keep things afloat. While they did not acquire much money, they built a loyal group of customers. More important, they earned the respect and trust of the tough neighborhood. When customers did not have enough money to pay for their food, my parents told them not to worry. Word spread, and the people of the neighborhood developed a deep fondness for them.

"Write me an IOU and keep it in the cash register. I'll pay you back on my next pay day," certain individuals insisted. The debt usually got paid. The neighborhood customers also earned my parents' regard.

Dad knew the community accepted his store when his customers raved to their family, friends, and church about the food at N&T. It became a common occurrence for different members of the same family to stop several times a week. Soon, we recognized the faces and names of regular customers and knew what they wanted to order.

There was Mr. Davis, who owned a tire shop nearby, who came every Friday to get a drum fish, cleaned and cooked. As soon as he entered the store, he would yell out to me, "Hey, Miss N&T, fix me up my usual."

A charming couple in their eighties came in together once a week. Dad called them "Mamma and Daddy," and they answered with, "Give Mamma the catfish strip, and Daddy wants the fried rice."

Dad came to know all the local ruffians over his sixteen years in business. He chased many of them off of the premises, but tension did not grow between them. Instead, a bond between Dad and the neighborhood troublemakers developed. Perhaps they recognized a kinship. They grew up and brought their own kids back to introduce them to my parents.

"Remember, Pops, when I came in here after school and smeared ketchup on your counter and floors? You chased me out with a broom!"

There were some young former convicts who frequented the store. N&T Seafood became one of their first stops after their release from jail.

"Hey, Pops! I missed your food," a man with a teardrop tattooed near the outer edge of one of his eyes said.

"Where you been, young man?" Dad asked.

He looked at Dad with a sly smile. They both knew where he had been. Both sides may have started out spatting, but over several years, the young customers came to call my parents "Pops" and "Mom." When they came through the door, the first thing they'd ask before placing their order was to speak to Pops, and they waved to Mom in the kitchen. Dad called the males "young man" and females "young lady," no matter their age.

The customers made the little family business the local Mom and Pop store, a fixture in the neighborhood. When my parents went shopping at the local market for supplies, the cashiers and stockers called out to them like family, "Hey, Pops! Hey, Mom! I'll be by the store later."

Our place held the reputation of being one of the longest operating family-owned stores in the neighborhood. More astonishing to other merchants, N&T Seafood under Dad's watch had the distinction of being the only business in the area that was never robbed in its sixteen years. Dad guessed that a few of his customers may have committed some of the other area crimes, but when they sauntered into N&T Seafood they paid their $2.99.

CHAPTER 25

The Three Letters

DAD HAD A KNACK for making friends, even the four-legged kind. Every night, at closing time—like clockwork—the stray cats and dogs appeared by the dumpster in the back of the store. They waited for the leftover pieces of fried fish that he saved for them. The hungry dogs wagged their tails when they saw Dad step out with garbage bags in both hands. The cats rushed to him and swirled their bodies against his legs. He patted his four-legged friends and pulled out a piece of fish for each of them. After the animals licked up the last crumbs from the ground, Dad stuck out his hand and the dogs placed their paws on his palm as if to say, "Thank you." Sometimes, Dad was able to get the cats to shake his hand as well.

I watched Dad's nightly ritual with the stray canines and felines throughout my college years. If I was not in class or studying, I was working at N&T Seafood. I also took an additional job in a biochemistry lab during college to earn extra money to help my parents. This did not leave me much time for a social life, but that did not bother me. Both Mom and Dad encouraged but never placed any academic or work pressure on me.

One evening in my final year of college, I watched from the back door of the shop. The sight of my father petting the cats and dogs made me smile at the sweet ending to a long and exhausting day. I noticed that the folds of skin on his face sagged lower by the end of the day. His back hunched over slightly, aching from lifting boxes of fish, cases of soft drinks, and sacks of flour. He rubbed a shoulder to ease the pain that accumulated after chopping dozens of fish parts. I knew that both my parents worked hard, and I wished life were easier for them.

Dad entered the store after the garbage was dumped and his furry friends were fed. With Mom standing nearby, I waited for him. I had waited the whole day to show him three letters. I had actually anticipated this moment much longer —four years. During that time, I kept my dreams to myself and plugged along. The first was a dean's letter; the second had an address from Des Moines, Iowa; the third came from the US Army. I showed him the first letter, which acknowledged that I would graduate college that semester with magna cum laude honors. The second letter offered acceptance to medical school in Des Moines, Iowa, in the fall. Finally, I smoothed out the folded creases of the third letter and laid it flat in front of Dad.

"This last one is an award for a military scholarship to pay for all four years of medical education in return for four years of service after I graduate. A good deal, huh?" I asked, gauging his reaction.

Dad thought it was more than a good deal but felt too overwhelmed to speak at that moment. He asked for the

letters and went to a corner in the back shed to study them
by himself. He found a bucket and turned it over to sit next
to the counter where he gutted fish. He read the letterheads
but did not go further. His eyes watered, and a smile crept
over his face. He looked at the first two letters and remembered consoling me when I flunked kindergarten and fell
behind in school. He folded the two letters and returned
them to their envelopes. He lingered with the third letter
and gently traced the US Department of Defense emblem
at the top. He could feel his nose warming and gave it a
quick wipe before it dripped like his eyes. Since his arrival
in America, Dad wanted to give back as much as he had
gained. Now, through his children, he saw that American
dream realized.

He jumped up from the bucket stool like he was a young
lieutenant again. He walked back to the kitchen area with
a spring in his steps. He found me sweeping the floor and
Mom scrubbing the cutting boards and kitchen utensils in
the sink.

"Looks like we have a road trip to Des Moines," Dad
announced with an excited sparkle in his eyes.

SIXTEEN YEARS HAD PASSED since
we left Nebraska for Texas. In summer 1998, we headed
back to the Midwest. Memories raced through Dad's
mind during that long drive to Des Moines. So much had
changed since the first time he took to the roads in that
blue Ford station wagon. Back then, he only had two small
children and everything he owned was packed in the car.
Life brought new changes, but the rolling green hills and
sea of cornfields along the highways of the heartland were
still there to welcome us back.

My parents did their best to set up home for me in the
small apartment across from the school. We bought a

I receive my captain's bars, in the same week of getting my medical degree. (Courtesy of Tran B. Quan)

folding card table at Walmart to use as a dining table. We found a nice wooden chair and study table at a garage sale. Someone in the building had thrown out an old couch, still in decent condition, that found a new home in my apartment. When it came to a bed, my parents insisted on a new twin mattress and box spring. Like good Asian parents, they could not leave until they made sure there was a bag of rice in the cupboard that would last for at least a semester. They found the only Asian market in Des Moines at the time and stocked my kitchen with fish sauce, soy sauce, and noodles. Before going back to Houston, my parents gave the apartment a thorough cleaning and cooked enough food to last several weeks.

Even Little Hen, who came along, gave me some good advice before she left. She told me, "Be nice and polite to everyone."

"Yes, ma'am." I jokingly smiled with my head lowered, shoulders slumped like I was back in elementary school again, being punished for misbehaving.

Four years later, in 2002, my family returned to Des Moines to attend my graduation. I was the first in my family to become a doctor. Upon graduation from osteopathic medical school, I was commissioned as a captain in the United States Army as part of my military scholarship commitment. The school held an additional commissioning ceremony for several of its graduating students with the same military scholarship.

"So help me God," I repeated the last line of the oath of commissioned officers with eight other graduating students in front of an auditorium. The ceremony's senior officer, also a military doctor, called my parents to the front of the room to pin my captain's bars. Dad took the two silver bars and fastened them to my jacket. Then he stood back to look at me in my Army uniform. He leaned in to give me a hug and whispered, "Everything that we had gone through to get to this point has made the journey worthwhile."

CHAPTER 26

Honest Labor

THE SPLASH FROM A brown-feathered pelican broke the silence around me as it dived into the reef water of John Pennekamp State Park and emerged with a flailing fish. It devoured the fish with one gulp and flew off. The bird reminded me that it was time to leave. I turned around to head back and found Dad walking toward me.

"How carefree," Dad said, pointing to the bird. "It swoops down for its meal and flies away."

We walked back to the car together and saw General Di talking to a park visitor wearing a Vietnam veteran cap. General Di stuck out his hand to wrap up the conversation. The American veteran, instead, gave General Di a swift salute. Without missing a beat, the general stood straight as a flagpole and saluted back.

I asked Dad, "I wonder if this veteran knows that he's speaking to a former South Vietnamese general?"

"Probably not," Dad said with a casualness that underscored the humble trait he knew the general possessed.

General Di kept his rank and past to himself, rarely revealing it to new acquaintances. He had to leave his past behind in Vietnam to navigate a new life in America. Unlike the lightsome pelican, General Di had to toil again to retrieve his freedom, but this time it was at his choosing.

ON JULY 4, 1993, red, white, and blue flags hung on porches, and smaller flags, poked into the ground, lined the front yards of homes in the Orlando neighborhood that General Di passed through on his first day to work. Just within a few months of arriving in America, General Di found a job at Dobbs Airline Catering. A friend who worked at Dobbs introduced him to the manager but felt uneasy about the position, knowing the general deserved better. General Di told his friends and family, "There is no shame with honest work."

With the car's window rolled down, General Di caught a whiff of meat grilling. His younger brother drove while he admired the patriotic display. The American flag made him feel protected. It gave him a chance to start over. At age sixty-two, when most people neared retirement, General Di had to rebuild his life.

Despite having served more than twenty years of active duty in the military, not including the seventeen years of captivity, General Di had neither the security of a pension nor been granted the benefits of the Veterans Administration that his American allies received. Yet, he still felt grateful. And while most people relaxed on the holiday, he worked. Without any self-design, events in his life, he mused, seemed to fall on meaningful dates.

Freedom for General Di meant financial as well as personal independence. General Di wanted to work not just for money. He wanted to work because he still felt productive and healthy. The years of deprivation in the concentration

General Di pedals a pushcart around Orlando's Splendid China Amusement Park selling refreshments during his first year in America in 1993. (Courtesy of General Di's family)

camps kept him slender and tough. His body became accustomed to hard physical labor.

General Di arrived early on his first day and went straight to the production area where an assembly line with food trays waited. Each tray had to be prepared in the exact same way. Before the afternoon break, he got into the groove of placing food into its exact order for each tray at a rapid pace. At lunch, the cook on staff prepared a full-course meal for the workers, free of charge. General Di sat by himself in the lunchroom and enjoyed his hot meal, a luxury for honest labor he had not known after 1975.

His coworkers thought the new employee seemed like a pleasant older man who didn't talk much but smiled when their eyes met. They didn't have time to get to know him, however. After six months at Dobbs, General Di found a higher paying job at Splendid China Amusement Park. This time, he drove to the new job in his own car, a used, two-door red Honda Civic hatchback, which he purchased with the help of his children. A little over six months after coming to America, General Di had a job, a car, and, most important—his freedom!

Every day, at the amusement park, he pedaled a bicycle attached to a pushcart that resembled a three-wheel cyclo taxi in Vietnam. He filled the pushcart with snacks, coffee, and sodas to sell as he pedaled around the theme park, passing miniature-scale versions of the Great Wall and the Forbidden City.

The long-sleeved uniform became soaked with sweat as General Di pedaled the red pushcart around and around the theme park during the height of summer. The physical work helped him maintain his slender frame. He felt strong and independent. General Di held his head high and beamed a wide smile when handing canned sodas to customers. Each mile that he biked was like another mile away from the prison cell. The communist chant of "Labor is glory" that rang in his ears for almost two decades became dulled by a new sense of freedom found in the honest endeavor of his choice.

When one job ended, he went on the hunt for the next, refusing to take a break. He worked at Splendid China for one year until the theme park closed. After Splendid China, he bussed tables and washed dishes at an Orlando restaurant. Then a friend who worked at Disney World told him to apply to Epcot. They hired him at age sixty-four.

General Di folded t-shirts and restocked the merchandise at Mouse Gear. He rarely missed work and was a supervisor's dream. His familiar and hearty laughter rang out often in the Disney shop and kept his colleagues' spirits buoyant. But there was a dignified, pleasant aloofness about General Di that made him likable, yet hard to know completely.

After work, he attended Valencia Community College. He found a seat in the night class that had working students like himself, but they were the ages of his children and grandchildren. When the instructor launched into a conversation in French, most of the students taking the introductory French language class sat with blank stares. But General Di could carry on a fluent conversation with the instructor. He wanted to teach French and approached a college counselor about working toward a bachelor's degree. This endeavor, however, did not materialize due to his desire to be financially independent, which required him to continue working full time.

While General Di's desire to obtain his American college degree was not realized, his children received their education and became productive adults, contributing to their American community just as he had dreamed while in the dark prison cell. His youngest son, Vince, became a software engineer and designed device simulations for Chinook helicopters. General Di's daughter, Que Huong, worked in real estate. General Di's oldest son, Tri, served as an electrical engineer for a branch of Lockheed Martin in Taiwan, specializing in the mechanics of Apache helicopters. His middle son, Toan, was a restaurant manager who sadly passed away from heart disease at age forty-five.

General Di found stability at Epcot and worked there for twelve years until his retirement. He stayed busy in retirement, attending rallies and speaking engagements at the request of the Vietnamese communities in Florida. General Di had a hard time declining requests even when they left him little time for himself. He could not turn down the call to remind Vietnamese expatriates and first-generation Vietnamese Americans about the cost of freedom. He wanted to honor the memory of the ARVN soldiers. He told the crowd, "Teach your children to become productive citizens and contribute something good. We owe much to this country."

When he did have time to himself, General Di sat contently with a book on military history, while classical music drifted in the background. If a concerto by Beethoven or Mozart was not playing, *La Vie en Rose* floated through the house. That was his favorite song, which translates as "life in rosy hues." The title translation could be interpreted as looking at the world through distorted lenses. But the song, for him, delivered the kind of positive optimism that carried him through rough times. Plus, it reminded him of a nostalgic time in his youth when he heard it sitting in a café along the tree-lined boulevard in Vietnam.

ONE DAY IN 2014, as Edith Piaf belted out the melodic French tune on the stereo, General Di picked up his phone to answer a call. He recognized the incoming number from Texas, a number given to him by an Orlando reporter who wrote a story about the general in a Vietnamese magazine. The reporter told General Di that a former ARVN soldier in the 9th Infantry Division, Le Quan, who lived in Texas, had read the article and wanted to reconnect with him. General Di consented and gave out his personal cell phone number.

The memories of his army buddies and General Di had never left Dad. Competing thoughts occupied his mind while he tried to carve out a life in America. But during quiet moments, the haunting memories of Dad's past would sneak back. When Dad discovered the article on General Di, he felt like a gutsy twenty-two-year-old lieutenant again and did not hesitate to retrieve a piece of his past.

The unexpected reunion and friendship between the general and the soldier received a second chance to blossom in 2014.

"Hello, General," Dad said with a crack in his voice from nervous anticipation. "This is Le."

"Call me *Anh Ba*, Younger Brother," General Di reminded with the same gentle chuckle that Dad remembered. Dad's tension melted away like it had when he first met General Di over four decades ago. The polite five-minute chat did not end their discourse after the two hung up. General Di rang Dad occasionally to share an amusing joke, and Dad felt comfortable enough to call the general up to talk like old friends about all kinds of "nonsense from heaven to earth."

On one call, Dad learned that General Di had to give up his dream to teach French so that he could continue to work. He told General Di, "You have been a teacher and mentor to thousands of soldiers, officers, and me." He added, "Anh Ba, I would like to come and visit you in Orlando soon."

"I welcome your visit, Younger Brother," General Di answered.

"If you still have your helicopter, do you think I can get a ride from Texas to Florida?" Dad joked. A stream of laughter flowed from the other end of the phone line.

CHAPTER 27

The Destination

WE CONTINUED OUR ADVENTURE on the Overseas Highway. The 113-mile road would take us from Florida's mainland to Key West, the last island in the chain of islands that is the southernmost tip of the continental United States. The highway seemed endless, surrounded on both sides by water, connecting one Key island to the next. On some stretches, it felt like we were driving into the sea with only wispy white clouds on the horizon. The mile markers toward Key West shortened with each Key that we crossed.

Our trip covered half the length of the Florida peninsula, almost 400 miles. During the rest stops, park visits, restaurant breaks, and hours on the road, our talks revealed two longer journeys: Dad's and General Di's.

"My life is nothing remarkable," Dad said. "I was just

among the many caught up by war. I did my best. The heroes are ones like General Di,"

"The heroes are the soldiers who fought and died for the cause of freedom," General Di reminded him. "The rest of us are survivors."

Everyone in the van agreed. We all shared a much bigger story, one long past and almost forgotten by time.

The van kept up its steady pace until the mile marker read zero and we passed a sign that read, "Welcome to Key West, Paradise USA."

Planted rows of mature coconut trees lined the streets, and fiery red-orange blossoms from the poinciana trees dotted the island. Key West had the vibe of a colorful Bahamas village.

Arriving at mid-afternoon, Cousin Hung continued to drive to the beach side of town. We admired the white sand and turquoise water that led out to the Gulf of Mexico. Then Cousin Hung turned onto an avenue leading to the main district.

The streets got narrower as the van made its way into the hub of town. On each side of the boulevard, small bungalow homes with white picket fences draped with ivy stood harmoniously next to bars and souvenir shops. People on bicycles and scooters cruised along, taking their time and soaking in the sun.

Cousin Hung circled the blocks looking for a parking spot in the charming but crowded town square. Everyone shuffled out of the car when he found a parking spot. We joined the tourists peering into the shops full of sweets, cigars, clothes, and crafts. Dad stayed behind with General Di. He bought himself and the general a piña colada from a refreshment stand. They sipped on the cold beverages and watched people strolling by draped in beachwear, sandals, and sunglasses.

Dad took a long sip from his piña colada and said, "It's missing something." He checked to make sure Mom was not within earshot.

"You are amusing, Younger Brother." General Di shook his head with a grin.

"It's a virtue that has helped me survive," Dad asserted. "What kept you going during your darkest times, Anh Ba?"

Without hesitation, General Di answered, "God and family."

I caught Dad's question and the general's answer as I walked toward them. I was not surprised by their revelations. No doubt they were different, and they knew it. Yet, they respected one another's traits. By this point on the trip, I could appreciate that their polar-opposite personalities enabled each to confront the unique set of challenges that life threw at them.

Learning the details of my father's past, especially, helped me to understand the multifaceted dimensions of his character. While he is fun-loving, there is a deep scar that war carved into him. He is my father, but he was also a son, a soldier, and a survivor.

When his belly grumbled, Dad waved to the rest of the group, signaling everyone to return. "Where are you treating us for dinner, Daughter?" Dad half teased.

"How about a sunset dinner cruise?" I offered, holding an advertisement flyer I found tacked on the walls of one of the souvenir shops.

Standing between Dad and General Di, I took each by the arm and walked together with them to the car. That moment, for me, felt like finding the last two pieces of a puzzle that merged to form one picture. It felt right.

We headed to the port and boarded a commercial yacht with a group of tourists. With the sun bearing down and calypso music playing on the upper deck, the boat sailed out into the water. Dad and the others made a beeline for the lower deck to cool down before dinner was served.

On a beach in Key West with two ARVN patriots: General Di and Dad. (Courtesy of Tran B. Quan)

Dad sat down at the table and touched the fresh-cut flower centerpiece. Its light fragrance was drowned by an even more pleasing scent for Dad: food cooking! He could smell savory aromas mingling together before the meal arrived.

When dinnertime approached, the staff carried out silver trays and placed them in rows on top of two tables. The servers lifted the covers to reveal a buffet of roasted pork, grilled chicken marinated in pineapple, fried fish, black beans and rice, deep-fried sweet plantain, and an array of salads and vegetables. Dad got in line first while General Di stood behind the group with me. Dad piled his plate with meats and a few sweet plantains; he skipped the vegetables. General Di scanned the selections and scooped a modest portion of each item.

Dad (left) and General Di (right) watch the setting sun on the Key West
horizon, 2015. (Courtesy of Tran B. Quan)

Famished, we leaned into our plates, gobbling the repast as the sun's evening rays burst through the lower deck windows.

"My eyes are bigger than my tummy," Dad admitted, trying to finish the food on his plate. He hated to waste food, ever since his days in the communist prisons. Starvation taught him that lesson. Yet, he could not help the impulse to pile on more than he could eat. He looked over at General Di who methodically cleared every scrap of food from his plate and went for seconds. Dad knew that General Di also hated to waste food.

When dinner ended, Dad and General Di wandered outside to the back of the boat. The evening sky lit with a burst of orange, red, and purple. The two stood side by side, leaning against the boat's rail. The cool evening gulf breeze gently ruffled their shirts. They watched the sailboats in the distance drift toward the sinking sun. Each man was lost in his own thoughts, staring at the brilliant splash of fiery colors across the sky. The blazing hues mellowed into pale shades of evening lavender and gray.

Dad said to General Di, "It has been a long journey."

Dad never imagined, as a penniless immigrant so many years ago, that he would be so richly blessed with opportunities that created a better life for his family. Or as a young lieutenant in Vietnam that he would later stand next to General Di and watch a sunset in a new homeland. He felt humbled.

General Di added, "I am a contented man."

No bitterness or regret lingered in the general's heart. His two prayers every day during those seventeen years of captivity came true: a return to freedom and reunion with his family. Out of his misery, his fortitude and resiliency prevailed.

Gazing at the two men just a few feet away, I felt grateful. In a blink, the last slice of the sun slipped below the horizon. The two men stood next to one another in peaceful silence.

Acknowledgments

I AM BLESSED TO know many new and old friends who have helped and inspired me to tell this story: Major General Tran Ba Di (ARVN, Ret.) and his family (Que Huong Tran, Vince and Lily Tran); Major General Le Minh Dao (ARVN, Ret.); General Arthur E. Brown Jr. (US Army, Ret.); Brigadier General John (Dai Uy "Nick") Nicholson Sr. (US Army, Ret.) and Mrs. Sophie Nicholson; Lieutenant Colonel Harry (Dai Uy "Mac") McFarland (US Army, Ret.) and Mrs. Rosalie McFarland; Lieutenant Colonel Thong Hong Tran (ARVN, Ret.); Khai Tran; Rebecca Nolen; Curt Locklear; Rajesh Thakur; Dr. Verena Hug; Thanh Du; Hung Nguyen; Hoang Nguyen; Thi Hoang; Boly Nguyen; Joyce and Neil Grothen; Joseph Craig; the two anonymous peer reviewers; and Travis Snyder, Christie Perlmutter, and the staff at Texas Tech University Press.

I owe a debt of gratitude to Dr. Lewis "Bob" Sorley, PhD, US Army Lieutenant Colonel (Ret.) and his wife Ginny, whose staunch support has allowed this book to come to fruition. Bob has used his talent and energy to champion my and many other South Vietnamese voices in remembering the Vietnam conflict. He is a friend to the South Vietnamese people.

To my parents, Le and Gia Quan, I am grateful for their belief and guidance. I feel equally blessed to have lived the story with them. I am proud to say that I am the daughter of the mischievous soldier who taught me about unconditional love.

I asked my parents and youngest sister to move in with me when Dad's health declined in 2016. Shortly thereafter, Dad was diagnosed with lung cancer. I told myself that I had to do everything I could to make Dad feel comfortable and secure during his battle. Some evenings I would come to his room, lay my head on his chest, and tell him, "Good night, Dad. I love you." He would pat the back of my head like I was a kid again and say, "I love you, too, flat head." It was an affectionate observation on the shape of my head that only Dad could make. Illness did not diminish his lightheartedness and joy.

On April 2, 2018, my father and I traveled to Orlando to be with General Di one last time. We stood in front of his casket. My father bowed his head and whispered, "Rest peacefully, Anh Ba." And he gave a final salute to his division commander.

On October 6, 2020, Dad took his final breath and was released from the suffering of cancer. In those last seconds, I witnessed the most serene look in my father's eyes. Words fail to describe the pain and beauty of that moment.

At Dad's memorial, I stood in front of the urn that contained his ashes and saluted my father.

TRAN B. QUAN

Bibliography

Email interviews
Tran, Khai. November 21, 2018.
Tran, Vince, Email references to author, September 18, 2017.

In-person interviews
Du, Thanh. October 1, 2018.
Nguyen, Hung and Hoang, April 3, 2018.
Quan, Gia. September 9, 2017.
Quan, Le. July–October 2015; January-April, 2016; July–September; 2016; March–May, 2017; January–May, 2018; July–September, 2019.
Tran, Ba Di. July 7, 2015; August 6, 2016; June 23, 2017.
Tran, Que Huong. June 23, 2017.

Telephone interviews
Brown, A. July 31, 2017.
Le, Minh Dao. January 3, 2018.
McFarland, H. August 4, 2017.
Nicholson, J. July 29, 2017.
Tran, Ba Di. April 16, 2017.
Tran, Thong. November 5, 2018.
Tran, Vince, and Lily Tran. August 18, 2017

Other sources

"Agent Orange." 2019. http://www.history.com/topics/
vietnam-war/agent-orange.

"American Funds for Czechoslovak Refugees Inc 1948–
1980." Retrieved 2017, http://www.afcsls.org/docu-
ments/AFCR.pdf

"Army of the Republic of Vietnam." Retrieved
2018, http://en.m.wikipedia.org/wiki/Army_of
the_Republic_of_Vietnam.

Dooley, Thomas A. *Deliver Us from Evil*. New York: Farrar
Straus & Giroux, 1956.

"The Fall of Saigon." Retrieved 2018, https://en.wikipedia.
org/wiki/Fall_of_Saigon.

"The Flag of South Vietnam." Retrieved 2018, http://
en.m.wikipedia.org/wiki/Flag_of_South_Vietnam.

"Former Chairman of Joint Chief General John Vessey
dies at 94." Retrieved 2018, https://apnews.com/
article/8cafd66326ad44a4a758b62094ecddb6

Gannon, Barbara A. "An Oral History of MG Di Ba
Tran [Senior Officer Oral History Program]." Oral
History Collection (U53.2T7322016, Tran, Di, Ba_
SOOHP_2014). US Army Heritage and Education
Center, Carlisle, PA, February 21, 2014.

"Ham Tan/Conditions in Ham Tan Reeducation Camp.
1981. Manuscript/mixed material. Library of Congress,
www.loc.gov/item/powmia/pw058829/.

Haoues, Rachel. "1975 CBS News Footage Shows
Dramatic Evacuation of Saigon." Retrieved
April 30, 2015, https://www.cbsnews.com/new
s/1975-cbs-news-footage-shows-the-dramatic-evac-
uation-of-saigon/

"Heroes of the Republic of Vietnam Armed Forces."
https://vacusa.wordpress.com/2016/04/13/heroes-o
f-the-republic-of-vietnam-armed-forces/

"Hitting Sanctuaries: Cambodia." Retrieved 2018, https://

www.nationalmuseum.af.mil/Visit/Museum-Exhibits/
Fact-Sheets/Display/Article/196023/
hitting-sanctuaries-cambodia/

Langguth, A. J. "The Vietnamization of General Di." *New York Times*, September 6, 1970, 5, 38–39.

Llewellyn, Jennifer, Jim Southey, and Steve Thompson. "Dien Bien Phu." Alpha History. Accessed September 22, 2017, http://alphahistory.com/vietnamwar/dien-bien-phu

———. "French colonialism in Vietnam." Alpha History. Accessed January 7, 2019, http://alphahistory.com/vietnamwar/french-colonialism-in-vietnam

———. "Geneva Accords of 1954." Alpha History. Accessed July 18, 2017, http://alphahistory.com/vietnamwar/geneva accords-of-1954.

———. "The Japanese occupation of Vietnam." Alpha History. Accessed January 10, 2018, http://alphahistory.com/vietnamwar/japanese-occupation-of-vietnam

———. "The Tet Offensive." Alpha History. Accessed September 15, 2019, https://alphahistory.com/vietnamwar/tet-offensive/

"Military Assistance Advisory Group." Retrieved 2018, https://en.wikipedia.org/wiki/Military_Assistance_Advisory_Group.

"Nam Ha Prison Camp in Phu Ly." 1981. [Manuscript/mixed material.] Library of Congress, https://www.loc.gov/item/powmia/pwmaster_23995/.

Nguyen, Qui Duc. "Revisiting Vietnam 50 Years After the Tet Offensive." January 2018,https://www.smithsonian-mag.com/history/revisiting-vietnam-50-years-after-tet-offensive-180967501/

"Orderly Departure Program." Retrieved 2019, https://en.wikipedia.org/wiki/Orderly_Departure_Program

"Scorched-earth." Retrieved 2018, https://www.merriam-webster.com/dictionary/scorched-earth.

Sorley, Lewis. *A Better War: The Unexamined Victories and Final Tragedy of America's Last Years in Vietnam.* New York: Houghton Mifflin Harcourt, 1999.

"South Vietnamese Popular Force." Retrieved 2017, https://en.wikipedia.org/wiki/South_Vietnam_Popular_Force.

"South Vietnamese Regional Forces." Retrieved 2019, http://en.m.wikipedia.org/wiki/South_Vietnamese_Regional_Force.

"The Suicides on April 30, 1975." http://www.vietamericanvets.com/Page-Records-TheSuicides.pdf

Thi, Lam Quang. *The Twenty-Five Year Century: A South Vietnamese General Remembers the Indochina War to the Fall of Saigon.* Denton: University of North Texas Press, 2012.

Tran, Ngoc Thong, Le Dinh Thuy, Ho Dac Huan. *Luoc Su Quan Luc Viet Nam Cong Hoa.* San Jose, CA: Huong Que Publishing & Distributing Inc., 2011.

"Viet Cong." Retrieved 2017, https://globalsecurity.org/military/world/vietnam/viet-cong.htm

"Viet Minh Take Control in the North." Retrieved 2019, http://history.com/this-day-in-history/viet-minh-take-control-in-the-north

"Vietnam: U.S. Advisors 1955–1965." Retrieved 2018, https://olive-drab.com/od_history_vietnam_advisors.php#:~:text=Vietnam%3A%20U.S.%20Advisors%201955%2D1965&text=Its%20mission%20was%20to%20supervise,to%20combat%20Viet%20Minh%20forces.

"Vietnamese Boat People." Retrieved 2019, https://en.wikipedia.org/wiki/Vietnamese_boat_people.

"Vietnamese National Army." Retrieved February 27, 2019, http://en.m.wikipedia.org/wiki/Vietnamese_National_Army.

"Vietnam War Dictionary RVNAF." Retrieved 2021, https://www.vietnamgear.com/dictionary.

"Vietnamization." Retrieved 2019, http://www.history.com/topics/vietnam-war/vietnamization.

Index

Note: Entry numbers in italics refer to images.

advisor(s), 88–90, 92, 95, *97*, 99, 101, 103, 212
Agent Orange, 58, 62
AK-47, 52, 134
American dream, 222, 224–25, 227, 232, 241
American Fund for Czechoslovak Refugees (AFCR), 171–74
Amnesty International, 121, 214
April 30, 108–9, 114–15, 121, 139, 220
Army of the Republic of Vietnam (ARVN), 5, 25–26, 31, 35, 45, 51–52, 58, 77, 87–89, 92, 95–96, 99, 101–2, 105, 109, 111, 114, 128, 139, 211, 213, 248–49, 254, 257
Australia, 164–65, 167

Bangkok, Thailand, 167–68
"boat people," xi, 156, 219

booby traps, 55, 57, 132
brick factory, 21, 27, 119
Brown, Arthur E., Jr, 99, 101, 257

California, 48–49, 170, 175, 220
Cambodia, 85, 87, 89, 101, 172
Camp Pendleton, California, 49, 215
Can Tho, Vietnam, 20, 94, 114–16, 120
Canada, 164, 166–67
Cang Long District, 99
Cavender, James, 88
Childress, Richard T., 212

Chinese immigrants, 175
Chuck, Mr., 183–86
Civil Guard and Self Defense Corps (CG/SDC), 92
civil war, 24
Cold War, 171
Collège Le Myre de Villers, 41

Compaq, 7, 201
Connant, Frank D., Colonel, 89
Cousin Hung, 16–18, 27, 36–38, *38*, 50, 81, 104, 150, 206, 222, *224*, 252
crabbing, 188–89, 200
Cushman, John, 96, 212

Da Lat National Military Academy, 31, 43–44
Dao, Le Minh, 128–30, 208, 210–13, 216–17, 257
de Tassigny, Jean Joseph Marie Gabriel de Lattre, 42
Des Moines, Iowa, 240–43
developmental disability, xii, 196
Di, Tran Ba, General, xi, 5, 8–17, 35–50, *38*, *47*, 77, 81–98, *97*, 101–9, 112–15, 120–29, 150, 169, 206–9, 212–20, *224*, 244–58, *246*, *254*, *255*
Diem, Ngo Dinh, 44
Disney World, 247
Du, Thanh, *38*
Duc Hoa, 45

15th Regiment, 51, 59
fishing boat, 115, 140, 151–54, 156
Florida, 12, 14, 16, 36, 38, 96, 102, 104, 131, 150, 220, 223, 248, 250–51
Ford station wagon, 7, 184, 205, 241
Fort Benning, Georgia, 48–49

Fort Myer, Virginia, 90, 96
IV Corps, 101, 105, 114, 211
France, 45, 166
French colonialism, 261

Galveston, Texas, 199–200
Geneva Accord, 24, 92
Germany, 97, 166
Giai, Do Ke, 217
Grandfather Luong, 21–23, 28–29, 32–33, 66, 116, 119, 133, 145, 147–49, 151–52
Grothen, Neil, 179–80, 182, 186, 257
Grothen family, *180*

Ha Tay Province, 122, 215
Hai, Nguyen Van, 63, 77–80, 84–86, 169
Harper, Douglas P., 215, 217, 220
Hastings, Nebraska, 174, 177–78, 180–83, 186–88
Ho Chi Minh City, 117, 217
Houston, Texas, 7, 12, 192–93, 199, 203, 224, 228, 232, 242
Hung, Le Van, 114
Huong, Que, 106, 214–15, 217–18, 248, 257
hut(s), 92, 132–33, 139, 141, 146, 157–61, *159*, 166–67, 224

International Refugee Organization (IRO), 171
Iowa, 92, 240

John Pennekamp Coral Reef

State Park, 222–24
Joint General Staff (JGS), 108

Key Largo, Florida, 206, 222, 224
Key West, Florida, 3, 14–16, 36, 206, 251–52, 254–55
Korean War, 31
Ky, Nguyen Cao, 128

Laem Sing Refugee Camp, Thailand, 159
land mines, 45, 54–55
Langguth, A. J., 87–89
Little Hen, 195–97, *224*, 224–25, 242

M1 Garand, 31
mangrove, 57, 122, 131–32, 144, 223
marble, 148, 151–52
Maryland, 186–88, 192, 200
McFarland, Harry ("Mac"), 47, *97*, 257
Mekong Delta, 44, 46, 52, 91–93, 96–99, 112, 122, 211, 223
Military Advisory Assistance Group-Vietnam (MAAG-V), 99
militiamen, 45–46, *47*
Minh, Ho Chi, 24, 109, 117, 140, 217
mortar, 26, 34, 70, 86, 95–96
My Tho, 41, 113

N&T Seafood, 228, *232*, 236–38, 240
Nam Ha, 122, 215–16
Nam, Nguyen Khoa, 114
National Training Center, 34, 105, 120
Nebraska, 173–75, 177, 180–81, 185, 241
Newsweek, 121
Nguyen Dinh Chieu, 39
Nicholson, John, Sr. ("Dai Uy Nick"), 92–97
9th Infantry Division (ARVN), 5, 35, 51, 75, 84, 87, 89, 113–14, 147, 249
North Vietnamese Army (NVA), 24, 26, 128, 138

Officer Candidate School (OCS), 101
Orderly Departure Program (ODP), 219
Orita, John, 174–75
Orlando, Florida, 3, 5, 13, 16, 36, 213–15, 220, 245–47, 249–50, 258
Orlando's Splendid China Amusement Park, *246*
Oversea Highway, *15*, 251

Phong Dinh Province, 92
Phu Quoc Island, 140
Piaf, Edith, 249
pirates, 111, 154–56
prison camp, xi, 118–19, 121, 123, 127, 131–32, 138, 140, 213, 216

Quan, Gia, 33, *38*, *65*, *67*, *159*, *224*, 257
Quan, Le, xi, *17*, *33*, *38*, *51*,

63, *65, 67, 159, 181, 224,*
249, *254, 255,* 257
Quan, Tran B., xi–xii, 15,
17, 33, 38, 51, 65, 67, 159,
180, 181, 180–81, *224,* 226,
232, *242, 254,* 254–55
Quan, Van, 145, *180,* 181–82,
185, 190, 194
Quang Trung National
Training Center, 105, 120

Rach Gia, Vietnam, 115, 151
Reagan, Ronald, 208,
212–13
Red Cross, 121, 214
reeducation camp, xi
refugee(s), 14, 108, 154,
156–61, 163–67, 171–73,
202–3, 225
Republic of Vietnam Armed
Forces (RVNAF), 25

Saigon, 23, 26, 42, 46, 48,
106–9, 112, 116–17, 120,
129, 150–51, 167, 173,
211–12, 217–18
San Francisco, California,
89, 170, 172–73, 181
Sarasota, Florida, 36, 38, 50,
81
Schutte, Larry, 179
scorched earth, 38
16th Regiment, 10, 62, 69,
71, 84–89, 111–12, 117,
147
Sorley, Lewis ("Bob"), 257
South Vietnamese prisoners,
210

T-L Irrigation Company,
183
Tampa, Florida, 17
Tan Ky, 216
Tan Son Nhut Air Base, 107
Tet, 25–27
Thailand, 115, 152, 154–
55, 157, 159, 167, 171,
223–24
Than, Le Van, 217
Thanh Cam, 216
Thieu, Nguyen Van, 108,
128
Thu Duc Military Academy,
30, 51
Time magazine, 121, 214,
217
Tra Vinh, 131, 144
trailer, 188–89, 201–4, 224–
25, 228
tuk-tuk, 116

US Army, xi–xii, 12, 49, 97,
102, 207, 240, 257
United Nations High
Commissioner for
Refugees (UNHCR), 154,
171, 219
United States, 14, 24–25, 45,
49, 89, 165–66, 209, 219,
243, 251
Utah, 172–73, 175

Vang, Tran Van, 39–40
Ven, Pham Van, 110
Vessey, John, Jr, 213
Viet Cong, 11, 22–24, 26–27,
34, 45, 52, 56, 58, 70, 72,
85, 88, 91, 95–98, 100–
101, 118–19, 132, 138,
144

Viet Minh, 24, 40, 42, 45
Vietnam National Army
    (VNA), 45
Vietnam War, xi, 8, 14, 37,
    166, 173
Vietnam–Cambodia border,
    85, 87
Vietnamization, 87, 89
Vinh Long, Vietnam, 18, 23,
    25–26, 33, 110, 116, 119,
    131

World War II, 23–24, 31, 38,
    46

Yen Bai, 122–23, 215

About the Author

T R A N B . Q U A N is a family physician. She has been the medical director at a state center for individuals with intellectual and developmental disability for over ten years. Before that, she served as an active-duty military physician in the US Army. She is honored and blessed to have cared for two populations that will always remain special and inspiring to her.